To Serve God and Mammon

Dilemmas in American Politics

Series Editor **L. Sandy Maisel,** *Colby College*

Dilemmas in American Politics offers teachers and students a series of quality books on timely topics and key institutions in American government. Each text will examine a "real world" dilemma and will be structured to cover the historical, theoretical, policy relevant, and future dimensions of its subject.

EDITORIAL BOARD

BOOKS IN THIS SERIES

To Serve God and Mammon: Church-State Relations in American Politics,
Ted G. Jelen

Money Rules: Financing Elections in America,
Anthony Gierzynski

The Accidental System: Health Care Policy in America,
Michael D. Reagan

The Dysfunctional Congress? The Individual Roots of an Institutional Dilemma,
Kenneth R. Mayer and David T. Canon

The Image-Is-Everything Presidency: Dilemma in American Leadership,
Richard W. Waterman, Robert Wright, and Gilbert St. Clair

Checks and Balances? How a Parliamentary System Could Change American Politics,
Paul Christopher Manuel and Anne Marie Cammisa

"Can We All Get Along?" Racial and Ethnic Minorities in American Politics, Second Edition, Updated,
Paula D. McClain and Joseph Stewart Jr.

From Rhetoric to Reform? Welfare Policy in American Politics,
Anne Marie Cammisa

Two Parties—Or More? The American Party System,
John F. Bibby and L. Sandy Maisel

Making Americans, Remaking America: Immigration and Immigrant Policy,
Louis DeSipio and Rodolfo de la Garza

The New Citizenship: Unconventional Politics, Activism, and Service,
Craig A. Rimmerman

The Angry American: How Voter Rage Is Changing the Nation, Second Edition,
Susan J. Tolchin

No Neutral Ground? Abortion Politics in an Age of Absolutes,
Karen O'Connor

Onward Christian Soldiers? The Religious Right in American Politics,
Clyde Wilcox

Payment Due: A Nation in Debt, a Generation in Trouble,
Timothy J. Penny and Steven E. Schier

Bucking the Deficit: Economic Policymaking in the United States,
G. Calvin Mackenzie and Saranna Thornton

Remote and Controlled: Media Politics in a Cynical Age, Second Edition,
Matthew Robert Kerbel

To Serve God and Mammon

Church-State Relations in
American Politics

Ted G. Jelen
University of Nevada at Las Vegas

Westview Press
A Member of the Perseus Books Group

322.10973
J48t

Dilemmas in American Politics

Copyright © 2000 by Westview Press, A Member of the Perseus Books Group

Published in 2000 in the United States of America by Westview Press, 5500 Central Avenue, Boulder,
Colorado 80301-2877, and in the United Kingdom by Westview Press, 12 Hid's Copse Road, Cumnor
Hill, Oxford OX2 9JJ

Visit us on the World Wide Web at www.westviewpress.com

Library of Congress Cataloging-in-Publication Data
Jelen, Ted G.
    To serve God and mammon: church-state relations in American politics / Ted G. Jelen
        p.   cm. — (Dilemmas in American politics)
    Includes bibliographical references and index.
    ISBN 0-8133-9988-2 (pbk.)
    1. Church and state — United States.   I. Title.   II. Series.

BR516 .J455 2000
322'.1'0973—dc21   00-035935

The paper used in this publication meets the requirements of the American National Standard for Per-
manence of Paper for Printed Library Materials Z39.48-1984.

10   9   8   7   6   5   4   3   2   1

Contents

Tables and Illustrations

Tables

Figures

Photos

Preface

In an important sense, I have been working on this book my entire life. It is no exaggeration to say that my life has been characterized by increasing exposure to religious diversity over time. During my forty-eight years as an observer of American religion, I have increasingly come to recognize the role of religion as a source of personal and communal identity as well as of interpersonal and political conflict. My personal and intellectual life has been characterized by increasing exposure to religious diversity, which in turn has shaped the ideas presented in this book.

I spent the first decade of my life in the comfortable ethnic and religious homogeneity of Chicago's southwest side. The city's Garfield Ridge neighborhood was uniformly white, Polish, and Catholic and was dominated by the benign omnipotence of St. Daniel the Prophet parish. My week, and that of everyone I knew, was organized around religious observance: novena[1] on Friday night, confession on Saturday night, and Masses on Sunday morning and the first Friday morning of every month. On Wednesday afternoon, Kinzie Elementary School emptied ninety minutes early, and the Catholic students who were enrolled in public school marched the three blocks to St. Daniel's, to take CCD (Confraternity of Christian Doctrine) classes under the supervision of the nuns. I later learned that this practice was upheld by a Supreme Court ruling stating that such released time was not a violation of the Establishment Clause. I played baseball in a league organized by the parish. The older kids went to dances sponsored by St. Daniel's—apparently designed to minimize the likelihood of an unfortunate marriage.

The Catholicism preached and practiced at St. Daniel's was of the pre–Vatican II, nonecumenical variety. St. Daniel's was among the last parishes to switch from the Latin Mass to the vernacular (alternating Masses in English and Polish). As a CCD student at St. Daniel's, I was taught that Roman Catholicism was the "one true Church," and was admonished to pray for "non-Catholics." My early religious training emphasized the importance of personal piety and morality. Significantly, the first U.S. presidential election of which I have clear memories is the 1960 election: We regarded the election of John F. Kennedy (the nation's first Catholic president) as a triumph of faith as well as politics. Nearly four decades later, my mother is still bitterly disappointed by the (apparently plausible) rumors of JFK's marital infidelity.

My sense of religious consensus and comfort came to an abrupt halt shortly after my tenth birthday, when my family moved from the southwest side of Chicago to the affluent western suburb of Hinsdale. In the fifth grade at Gower Elementary School, I had my first sustained encounters with Protestants and with the "new math." Although my experiences with the former were much more positive than with the latter, for the first time I was in the minority and felt like an outsider. For the first two years, I responded to my new environment with a drastic increase in personal religiosity and in the frequency of private religious devotions. Reciting the rosary and reading the Bible became part of my daily routine. My sense of religious alienation proved relatively short-lived, and I soon became quite comfortable in the undemanding Christian ecumenism of Chicago's western suburbs.

In 1970, I enrolled at Knox College in Galesburg, Illinois. This move resulted in my first sustained contact with Judaism. My roommate, Harvey Lipman of Evanston, Illinois, was the son of a Holocaust survivor. One warm day, in my freshman year, I caught a glimpse of the nine-digit number branded on Norman Lipman's left forearm. Harvey and Ken Sezer of Skokie, Illinois (a primarily Jewish suburb of Chicago, which later became the site of a Nazi rally), provided me with a serviceable vocabulary of Yiddish expressions, an appreciation for kosher food, and a rudimentary understanding of an important Western religious tradition. Our combined religious devotion did not deter us from devouring the odd pepperoni pizza on Ash Wednesday, or a ham-and-cheese submarine sandwich on Yom Kippur.[2] Nevertheless, our late-night "bull sessions" in the dorm gave me insight into another religious tradition as well as a deeper understanding of my own. Harvey, Ken, and I frequently observed that "there are no ex-Catholics or ex-Jews," by which we meant that one's religious upbringing placed an indelible stamp on one's personality.

The range of my religious exposure further increased during my graduate studies at Ohio State University, where I had my first sustained contact with Islam. A small minority of students from Iran, Egypt, Syria, and Nigeria became highly visible in the years immediately following the 1973 Yom Kippur War.[3] A clear fault line opened up between Jewish students (most of whom were U.S. citizens) and international students from the Arab countries of the Middle East. To my astonishment, the salience of the Arab-Israeli conflict seemed to permeate virtually every aspect of social life among graduate students in political science, history, and philosophy. Of course, what made this essentially religious conflict highly visible was a drastic increase in the price of gasoline and a sharp drop in the availability of petroleum-based fuels. Due to the Nixon administration's support of Israel, which made the latter's victory in the Yom Kippur War possible, the oil-producing states of the Middle East placed an embargo on oil exports to the

United States. The prices of gasoline and fuel oil quadrupled overnight, and the resulting inconvenience was often manifested in increasingly visible anti-Arab sentiment among Americans. Arabs—once a virtually invisible minority in the United States—became objects of prejudice, derision, and occasional violence.

Upon completion of my graduate studies, I secured my first full-time academic appointment—as an adjunct instructor, at Lamar University in Beaumont, Texas. My year-long stint in Beaumont expanded my religious education by bringing me into sustained contact with white evangelical Protestants (a group to which I have since devoted years of study). In certain quarters, the evangelical fervor of this East Texas community was laced with a strong dose of anti-Catholicism. Beaumont is located between two large concentrations of Catholics: Mexican-Americans to the west and south; and "Cajuns" (the descendants of French-speaking Canadians) to the east, in the southern half of Louisiana. A very small but highly vocal minority of Beaumont residents made it quite clear that they regarded Jefferson County (in which Beaumont is located) as an enclave of Protestant sanity surrounded by hostile, foreign-born (or at least, foreign-sounding) Papists.

I taught at Lamar during the 1978–79 academic year. This proved an important year in the formation of my intellectual agenda. At the same time as I was dealing with personal relations among people who were not members of my faith tradition (and who, in a few instances, were hostile to it), the insertion of religious values into politics was becoming an important national and international story. In late 1978, we learned that the College of Cardinals, for the first time in centuries, had elected a non-Italian pope, who even then was known for his outspoken anticommunism. (I was told that the election of John Paul II, a Pole, as head of the Papacy evoked much celebration at St. Daniel's.) This year also brought a successful Islamic revolution in Iran, in which the Ayatollah Khomeini replaced the Shah. During the same period, more than fifty Americans were taken hostage at the American embassy in Tehran by a group of students characterized as "Islamic fundamentalists." They were held for well over a year. The resulting U.S.-Iranian tension resulted in yet another oil embargo, which of course exacerbated anti-Iranian and anti-Arab (a distinction lost on most Americans) sentiment in the United States.

We also learned that the members of a Christian cult in "Jonestown" (a commune established by American evangelical James Jones in Guyana, South America) had committed mass suicide, apparently in response to the demands of their leader. Closer to home, a young Baptist minister named Jerry Falwell, who pastored the Thomas More Baptist Church in Lynchburg, Virginia, had founded an organization called the Moral Majority. Falwell, who had previously criticized the Rev. Martin Luther King for mixing religion and politics, sought to restore a religious and moral order to the United States, which Falwell argued had been fractured by the influence of "secular humanism." The combination of a religiously charged change in my personal circumstances and the highly visible role of religion in national and world affairs during this period had a permanent effect on my intellectual agenda.

After a few years as an academic nomad (including year-long stints at Illinois State University and the University of Kentucky), I returned to the western suburbs of Chicago, to take a position at Illinois Benedictine College (which later became Benedictine University). My religious education was advanced considerably during the sixteen years I spent at IBC. First, somewhat paradoxically, IBC provided my first exposure to polytheism. Benedictine University has a strong (and apparently deserved) reputation in the natural sciences and is known to provide excellent premedical training. While I was at Benedictine, the institution recruited a growing population of Hindu immigrants from India, who were attracted to BU's scientific reputation. Their exotic costumes, languages, customs, and holidays were a source of fascination for my faculty colleagues and of derision for many of our working-class Catholic students. More seriously, the presence of a substantial number of non-Catholic, non-Christian, and indeed, nonmonotheistic students posed a series of challenges for the traditions and curriculum of an institution with an explicitly religious mission. We were forced to debate questions such as the propriety of opening the school year with a ceremonial Mass, or the advisability of retaining a religious studies graduation requirement with such a religiously diverse student body. More generally, we continually wrestled with the question of how to balance the demands of a distinctively Catholic educational mission and a religiously multicultural student body.

A second facet of public religion became apparent to me while I was at Benedictine. My first years at IBC roughly coincided with the beginning of the Reagan administration. President Reagan was determined to alter drastically the direction of American domestic politics and foreign policy.

In response to statements and policies of the Reagan administration relating to the possibility of "limited" nuclear war, the need to free the Western hemisphere of the influence of communism, and the "wastefulness" of policies designed to assist the disadvantaged, the National Council of Catholic Bishops issued pastoral letters on nuclear war, U.S. policy in Central America, and capitalism in the United States. In all of these areas, the NCCB advanced strong arguments about the moral imperatives involved in such issues. Cardinal Joseph Bernardin of the Chicago Archdiocese articulated a Catholic position involving "a consistent ethic of life." Using the metaphor of a "seamless garment," Bernardin argued that the Church's traditional opposition to abortion (which the Reagan administration shared) was simply one aspect of a more general "pro-life" principle—a principle that also raised questions about the morality of warfare, capital punishment, and apparently uncharitable policies toward the poor. In sum, the Church in the early 1980s took a public stance that might be termed "prophetic": That is, the Church sought to provide a moral basis for political discourse. These activities occasioned public discussion about the merits of the bishops' substantive arguments as well as procedural questions about the propriety of public statements by religious bodies.

In 1997, I left Benedictine to chair the department of political science at the University of Nevada at Las Vegas. Living in the American West for the first time has put me into contact with yet another religiously distinctive group: members of the Church of Latter-Day Saints. Visitors to Las Vegas are frequently unaware of (or surprised by) the presence of such a large body of religious citizens in the morally relaxed atmosphere of southern Nevada. Nevertheless, Mormons have developed a distinctive subculture in the Silver State, and they constitute a group of voters that local candidates of both parties seek to cultivate. The Mormons with whom I have become personally acquainted are acutely aware of the history of religious persecution of their church—and of the current practice of some residents of Las Vegas of dropping the second "m" in the word *Mormon*.

This somewhat extended personal narrative is intended to illustrate a simple point. Over the span of my personal and intellectual life, I have been very impressed by the power of religious belief to shape, alter, and occasionally distort the practice of politics in the United States and elsewhere. In the pages that follow, I have attempted to present both sides of the "dilemma" posed by contemporary church-state relations in as even-handed a manner as possible. My editors at Westview inform me that for the most part, I have succeeded. However, I will reveal at this point that my bias runs toward a strongly "separatist" vision of the relationship between government and religion. This is not to deny the important contributions made by religion to political life. In the United States, the abolitionist, civil rights, and antiwar movements (among others) owe their existence and their success to the willingness of religious leaders and ordinary citizens to place their religious values above their narrow interests. In the area of international relations, I know of no credible account of the collapse of the Soviet empire and the apparent demise of communism in the West that does not credit Pope John Paul II with playing an important role. However, I am continually impressed with the power of religion to serve as a focal point for violent political conflict on the Indian subcontinent, in the Balkans, in the Middle East, in Northern Ireland, and elsewhere. I am grateful that religious violence is only an episodic phenomenon in the United States, and I believe that our system of church-state separation plays an important role in containing religious conflict. I hope the book you hold in your hands contributes to a deeper understanding of that system, and in some small way, to the attainment of public civility in a religiously diverse population.

Acknowledgments

A number of people made important contributions to this book. I would like to thank Leo Wiegman and Sandy Maisel for their wise counsel (and virtually infinite patience) in producing and revising this book; and Sandy, David McBride, and an anonymous third reviewer for detailed, insightful, and generous comments on my first draft. My friend, frequent coauthor, and even more frequent co-conspirator Clyde Wilcox provided (as always) a mixture of support, advice, and kind, constructive criticism. I am also indebted, more generally, to the merry band of scholars who study religion and politics. These people, whom Ken Wald habitually describes as "the usual suspects," know who they are, and they will recognize the thoughts put forth in this book as the latest installment in a conversation that has been going on continuously for more than a decade. I also thank Fr. Phillip Timko and Fr. David Turner at Benedictine University, and Mehran Tamadonfar at UNLV, for valuable insights into particular religious traditions; and Michael Bowers, for quick answers to my naive questions about various details of constitutional law.

Finally, as always, primary credit must go to Marthe Chandler, my beloved wife. Beyond being my lover, my best friend, and my eternal companion, Marty serves as my conscience and my intellectual blood bank. Her wide-ranging interests are an important source of intellectual breadth, which often provides a necessary counterpoint to my occasionally monomaniacal concentration on very narrow topics. In the bedlam that often characterizes my life, Marty is an island of sanity and serenity. She acts as a constant reminder of the things that are really important to me and stubbornly resists any inclination on my part to compromise either my priorities or my principles. For all this, and for her having put up with me for nearly two decades (and counting), I am extremely and eternally grateful.

Ted G. Jelen
Las Vegas, Nevada

Notes

1. Novenas are petitionary services to the Virgin Mary.

2. Ash Wednesday is the first day of Lent, the Christian season of atonement just before Easter. On this day, Catholics are expected to refrain from eating meat. Similarly, on Yom

Kippur, the Jewish Day of Atonement (which occurs in autumn), Jews customarily fast. Ham, and the combination of meat and cheese, are violations of kosher (Jewish) dietary regulations.

3. On Yom Kippur (a High Holy Day in Judaism), in 1973, Israel was attacked by Egypt, Jordan, and Syria. During the course of this conflict, Israel added to its territory the West Bank of the Jordan River, the Golan Heights (adjacent to Syria), and the Sinai peninsula. This Israeli territorial acquisition shaped politics in the Middle East during the last quarter of the twentieth century.

1

The Religion Clauses

Competing Religious Values

At this season of
THE WINTER SOLSTICE
may reason prevail.

There are no gods,
no devils, no angels,
no heaven or hell.
There is only
our natural world.
Religion is but
myth and superstition
that hardens hearts
and enslaves minds.

This sign depicts an alternative interpretation of the holiday season.
The religion clauses of the First Amendment protect conventional and
unconventional religious beliefs alike. (*Tribune* photo by Andy Manis)

Among the more prominent—and to some, surprising—characteristics of contemporary American politics is the frequency with which religious values and beliefs are voiced in the making of public policy. Despite the ostensible constitutional separation of church and state, and despite current political, social, and intellectual trends that suggest American public life is becoming increasingly secularized, conflict continually erupts between the realms of the sacred and the secular. This book provides fresh perspective on the origins and persistence of church-state conflict in American political culture, exploring these key questions: What is the nature of conflict over the proper political role of religion in the United States? What are the sources of this conflict? Why are issues of church-state relations such a persistent feature of U.S. politics? Can these issues be resolved in the foreseeable future? Should Americans even seek a clear-cut resolution to the uneasy relationship between church and state?

Pivotal to this discussion is the tension implicit between two clauses in the First Amendment to the U.S. Constitution that relate to religion: the "Establishment" and the "Free Exercise" clauses. Much of the conflict that characterizes religious politics in the United States is attributable to the fact that the **Establishment Clause** appears to guarantee freedom *from* religion, whereas the **Free Exercise Clause** seems to guarantee freedom *of* religion (Davis 1996). In other words, the Free Exercise Clause allows citizens to hold, act upon, and promote their religious beliefs. In contrast, the Establishment Clause may hold out the promise that such efforts will *necessarily* be unsuccessful in the realm of politics: A plausible albeit controversial reading of the Establishment Clause suggests that the clause is intended to protect citizens with divergent or nonexistent religious beliefs from the consequences of others' exercise of religious freedom. The Establishment and Free Exercise clauses, in offering seemingly contradictory guiding principles, have created a dilemma for judges and other public officials seeking to decide legal and policy questions involving religion.

In the last two decades of the twentieth century, political and legal controversies over the public articulation of religion were particularly evident. Even a casual observer could not have missed the mass media coverage of one or another political issue involving the relationship between church and state. Following are just a few examples culled from newspapers:

In Republic, Missouri, a lawsuit was filed against the city council, in an effort to have the city's logo changed. The logo contained, among other symbols, a line drawing of a fish, which opponents claimed was a "secret Christian symbol" dating from the second century A.D. and thus was violating the separation of church and state (Goddstein 1998).

In Brooksville, Alabama, the Rev. James Henderson sought the incorporation of his hamlet as a town with the King James Bible as its charter and the Ten Commandments as its ordinances. Rev. Henderson wished to "bring together the church and state," in an effort to "make life make sense for people." Proponents argued that a Bible-based town would represent a return to the spirit of the country's founding fathers (Bragg 1998).[1]

In an effort to provide choices for the parents of schoolchildren, the City of Milwaukee enacted a system based on tuition tax vouchers that could be used at private schools. In response to a lawsuit filed by **Americans United for the Separation of Church and State (AUSCS),** the Wisconsin Supreme Court ruled that the use of tuition tax vouchers to cover the costs of tuition in religious schools did not violate the constitutional separation of church and state, since the aid was not granted directly to religious institutions but to the parents of students at parochial schools. AUSCS announced its plan to appeal to the U.S. Supreme Court, and confidently predicted that the Wisconsin high court's ruling would be reversed (Cohen 1998; Raspberry 1998).[2]

A columnist urged passage of the Illinois Religious Freedom Act, arguing that contemporary constitutional law does not adequately protect religious freedom. To illustrate, he noted that under current court rulings, Roman Catholic priests might be required to testify in criminal matters concerning information obtained in the confessional. He suggested that government legally could invoke criminal sanctions against priests who maintained the absolute confidentiality of the sacrament of confession (McConnell 1998).

The National Conference of Catholic Bishops issued a set of "guidelines" for Catholic colleges and universities in the United States. These included the recommendations that a majority (at least) of faculty at such institutions be committed Catholics, that presidents of Catholic institutions take "an oath of fidelity and profession of faith," and that theology faculty seek certification from local bishops. Critics of the guidelines, among whom were many members of Catholic university faculties, wondered whether these principles were consistent with the norm of academic freedom and whether they would interfere with decisions involving hiring, promotion, and tenure (Steinfels 1999).

Mildred Rosario, a substitute teacher in a public school in the Bronx, New York, was dismissed from her position. After observing a moment of silence for a student who had recently drowned, Rosario had invited students not wishing to participate in a discussion about God to take a book to the back of the room. She then had asked the remaining students if any of them would like "to accept Jesus as their personal savior." She laid hands on the foreheads of students while praying aloud. When sanctioned for this activity, Rosario indicated that she had an obligation to continue to promote her choice of Pentecostal Christianity. Both New York Mayor Rudy Giuliani and House Speaker Newt Gingrich spoke out against her dismissal (Chapman 1998).

A U.S. district judge dismissed a lawsuit brought against Yale University by four orthodox Jewish students, who argued that Yale had violated their right of religious free exercise by forcing them to live in coed dormitories. The university requires most students to live on campus during their first two years. The students alleged that the coed dorms violated their religious liberty, in that the living arrangements violated their faith's demand that they practice "chastity" and "modesty" (see *Chicago Tribune* 1998).

The political expression of religious belief in the United States generally has evoked opposition and countermobilization. Religious activists often have been criticized for particular positions they have taken on matters of public policy. More generally, the propriety of religious involvement in the political process also has been questioned. Some observers have raised procedural objections to religiously motivated political activity, arguing that the nation's founders intended that there be "a wall of separation" (Thomas Jefferson's words) between politics and religion (Wills 1990).

In contemporary American politics, the topic of church-state relations seems to be raised most often by members of the **Religious Right**, which consists primarily of doctrinally conservative **evangelical Protestants** (see Wilcox 1992; and Wilcox, DeBell, and Sigelman 1999). Groups such as Christian Voice, Religious Roundtable, and **Moral Majority** articulated important connections between religious values and political issues during the 1980s. In 1988, the Rev. Marion "Pat" Robertson, an evangelical Christian television personality, made a serious though unsuccessful bid for the Republican presidential nomination. In the 1990s, religious-political groups such as the **Eagle Forum**, **Family Research Council**, and

Christian Coalition advocated positions that provoked debates about church-state separation. In the last third of the twentieth century, religiously based political advocacy tended to come from the theological and political right, and the Christian Right was an increasingly important component of the Republican Party's mass basis of support.

However, the promoters of religious values in the public sphere have not always been religious or political conservatives. Religious zeal, in large part, animated the abolitionist movement of the mid-nineteenth century; the temperance movement of the first third of the twentieth century; many of the reforms advocated by Progressives; the civil rights and antiwar movements of the 1960s and 1970s; and the more recent "pro-life" or antiabortion movement, which sprang up after the Supreme Court issued its historic decision in *Roe v. Wade*. Even this short list shows that religiously inspired movements have espoused a variety of actions based on diverse ideologies—an observation that subverts any attempt to directly connect religion (or particular religious traditions) with specific political stances. Many prominent political liberals of the twentieth century—for example, Martin Luther King, George McGovern, Jesse Jackson, and Andrew Young—had experience in the Protestant ministry. Furthermore, during the early years of the Reagan administration (early 1980s)—when the public advocacy of liberal principles was unpopular—the United States Catholic Conference spoke out against the mobilization of nuclear weapons and against U.S. military involvement in Central America, and in favor of substantial increases in government assistance to the poor (Jelen 1993).

In sum, the principle of church-state separation is far from self-evident. At various points in American history, sacred values have been advanced by citizens at all points of the political spectrum. Religion is not inherently "liberal" or "conservative" but generally promotes a set of values transcending the terms of contemporary political discourse. At the same time, although most religious organizations are not *primarily* political in nature, their activity may have a political component. Despite Jesus's admonition to "render unto Caesar that which is Caesar's, and unto God that which is God's," there are many areas in which both sacred and secular activists would claim authority.

Why the United States?

Although there is a political aspect to religion in many nations (see Jelen and Wilcox, eds., forthcoming), some aspects of the relationship between church and state in the United States appear unique. Arguments of **American exceptionalism** seem particularly plausible in the case of public religion. First, America is a highly

TABLE 1.1   Religious Observance and Belief in Selected Western Nations

	Church Attendance[1]	*Importance of God[2]*
Belgium	35	13
Canada	40	28
France	17	10
East Germany	20	13
West Germany	33	14
Great Britain	25	16
Iceland	9	17
Republic of Ireland	88	40
Northern Ireland	69	41
Italy	47	29
Netherlands	31	11
Norway	13	15
Spain	40	18
Sweden	10	8
United States	59	48

[1]Percent reporting attending religious services at least once a month
[2]Percent rating importance of God in one's life at 10, on a ten-point scale
SOURCE: Author's compilation from data in *World Values Study, 1990–1991*.

religious country. Whether one measures religion in terms of belief, public observance, or affiliation, the population of the United States is substantially more religious than that of any other industrialized nation (Wald 1997). Indeed, the United
States is an outlier in a commonly reported negative relationship between religiosity and modernization. The United States stands virtually alone as a nation with
both a highly modern economy and a highly religious population. One would expect religious issues to be more important in American politics than in other national political settings, because religion is relatively important to Americans.

As the data in Table 1.1 show, a substantial majority of Americans report attending religious services at least once a month. This figure exceeds all other
countries listed in Table 1.1, with the exception of the Republic of Ireland and
Northern Ireland, which are somewhat less industrialized than most other Western nations. Moreover, religious affiliation is an important source of national
identity for the Irish. Table 1.1 also shows that the attachment of importance to
God in one's life is more widespread in the United States than in any other nation
listed, including Ireland.

The extent of religious belief and practice appears to be a source of both cohesion and conflict in American politics. Because religious belief in general is so
widespread, the rhetorical symbols associated with support for religious faith are

extremely powerful. Few candidates running for public office would publicly identify themselves as atheists or agnostics. As I write, a number of potential presidential candidates of both parties are making public statements about the depths of their own religious beliefs, and suggesting ways in which religious organizations can contribute to the practice of democratic politics (Tumulty 1999; Tackett 1999).

However, identification with a specific religious tradition or theology has often been costly to particular candidates or organizations. The candidacy of Al Smith for U.S. president in 1928 is widely believed to have been doomed by Smith's Catholicism; and more than a generation later, in 1960, the Catholicism of John F. Kennedy was still an important enough issue to have a negative impact on his margin of victory in the presidential election (Converse 1966). Similarly, the outspoken evangelical Christianity of Jimmy Carter—termed "the weirdo factor" by Carter aide Hamilton Jordan (Witcover 1977)—became an important issue in the presidential election of 1976, when it appears to have cost Carter some traditional Democratic support among Roman Catholics. More recently, Religious Right organizations such as Moral Majority have been increasingly unpopular, even among their targeted constituencies (Wilcox 1992; Jelen 1991). Although a generalized support for religion seems necessary for political acceptability, public adherence to a specific religious tradition can occasionally result in political divisiveness.

The process of modernization clearly has not eradicated the importance of religion in American political and social life. However, it seems equally clear that the public face of religion has been altered substantially by contact with contemporary secular society.[3] The evolution of the modern nation-state created a serious competitor for religious authority and activity. The provision of social services such as education, health care, and charity, as well as the sanctioning of social institutions such as marriage and parenthood, which had long been within the province of religion, increasingly were taken over by national, state, and local governments. A "separation" of church and state is quite difficult when the jurisdictions of the two realms overlap to the degree that is apparent in contemporary American society. Indeed, much church-state jurisprudence is driven by the question of whether the authority of God or Caesar should trump when the obligations of citizenship and discipleship collide. As we will see in subsequent chapters, much of the conflict concerning the appropriate relationship between religion and government has arisen in policy areas dealing with government as the provider of services.

A second characteristic of American political culture that gives rise to church-state tension is the emphasis placed on **rights**. Many observers have suggested that an important source of American exceptionalism is the general agreement among

Americans on a public philosophy of Lockean individualism (Hartz 1955; Wills 1990). According to the English philosopher John Locke, and adherents of Lockean thought, such as Thomas Jefferson (the author of the Declaration of Independence), humans are naturally endowed with a private sphere in which government may not legitimately interfere. Rights exist within this zone of individual sovereignty, and are, in the words of Jefferson, "unalienable," which means that they cannot be taken away. In this conception, rights are nonnegotiable limitations on the power of government. Thus, if citizens can successfully assert rights, then they have identified an area in which the exercise of government power, no matter how wise and well-intentioned, is unacceptable (see Glendon 1991).

"Rights talk" in American politics is so ubiquitous that Americans tend to forget that governmental functions generally do not involve the exercise of individual rights. For example, most Americans would agree that citizens of the United States do not have a right to keep all of their income and do have an obligation to pay taxes. It is also generally understood that the precise level of taxation is best determined by the elected branches of government, which are responsible for ensuring that the government has the means necessary to fulfill its functions. If taxes were to become so high as to be unacceptably burdensome, or so low that the government was unable to provide essential services, one would expect the responsible public officials to suffer prompt electoral reprisal. In matters like taxation, which are outside the sphere of "rights," Americans commonly rely on the democratic process to translate public opinion into public policy.

In contrast, rights involve citizens' prerogatives that are outside the range of government intervention, and by extension, beyond the reach of popular majorities. One area of church-state relations that is repeatedly contested involves the question of a right to conduct organized prayer in public schools. For much of American history, it was customary for public schools to begin each day with an organized (usually Christian) prayer. In 1962, in the case of *Engel v. Vitale*, this practice was declared unconstitutional. Public opinion polls taken over the past half century have shown that most Americans approve of the idea of school prayer. If government decisions in this area were made democratically—by elected officials seeking to ensure their own reelection—prayer might still be a normal part of the daily scholastic routine. However, the courts have determined that citizens have a constitutional right *not* to have their children exposed to government-sponsored religious observances. Even if only a few parents object, the majority must give way before the successful assertion of such a right.

Since questions about the public role of religion involve the application of rights guaranteed by the Constitution, it follows that public policy in the church-state area is not subject to the will of a popular or a legislative majority. In the area of religion and politics, public officials are presumably motivated by some combination of their perceptions of what is politically popular and what is sound policy. However, because church-state issues are necessarily complicated by the assertion of different and competing rights, they inevitably pose questions of the legitimate power of government. In addition to the question of what government *should* do in a particular area, issues of rights involve the question of what governmental institutions *can* do within the limits of their legal power. The complex interplay between politics and rights implicit in questions of church-state relations has mandated that such questions be decided by the courts—the branch of government least affected by public opinion and popular sentiment. Issues of "church vs. state" are often framed in terms of a conflict between democracy and personal freedom—which explains the high emotions surrounding their debate.

The Religion Clauses: Interpretations and Tensions

The specific source of the persistent *legal* conflict over church-state relations in the United States is the fact that the relationship between the sacred and the secular is a matter of constitutional principle. That is, religious freedom is thought to be so fundamental as to be a part of the basic social contract. Indeed, many observers have noted that freedom of religion, as defined by the Establishment and Free Exercise clauses, is the first right listed in the Bill of Rights (see Wood 1990). The constitutional context of church-state relations in the United States has its source in the following language in the First Amendment: "Congress shall make no law respecting an establishment of religion, or prohibiting the free exercise thereof." The Establishment and Free Exercise clauses have provided the legal setting within which church-state relations have been contested in American politics. Church-state relations become a *problem* for the American system because there is little agreement on the spare language used in the religion clauses of the First Amendment. There is no general agreement on what sorts of government practices would or would not constitute proscribed "establishment" of religion; nor is the question of the proper scope of the Free Exercise Clause close to being settled. Clearly, not all religious practices are constitutionally protected, but discerning the precise point at which religiously motivated citizens and groups can exercise religious rights that government is obliged to accept has been a frustrating, and generally futile, task.

People generally adopt one of two basic positions toward the Establishment Clause. These positions might be termed **accommodationism** and **separatism** (Jelen and Wilcox 1995, 3). An accommodationist might argue that the proper relationship between church and state is one of benevolent neutrality, in which the Establishment Clause is taken to mean that government is simply prohibited from extending preferential treatment to any *particular* religion. However, this stance of nonpreferentialism is not thought to proscribe government support to religion in general. Government, from an accommodationist standpoint, is not required to be neutral between religion and irreligion.

Accommodationism appears to be based on two important assumptions. First, accommodationists tend to believe that religion has beneficial consequences for the social order. Religion provides a nonarbitrary code of moral human behavior that limits the scope of political conflict (Reichley 1985). Second, religion is regarded by accommodationists as a source of social cohesion. That is, differences between religious denominations are perceived as distinctions of doctrine, which do not typically result in different prescriptions for or proscriptions of human behavior (see Tocqueville 1945; Kirk 1986; and Jelen and Wilcox 1995). In the United States, a "Judeo-Christian tradition" is thought to provide a moral basis for political life—what some analysts have described as a "sacred canopy" beneath which political affairs can be conducted (Berger [1967] and Neuhaus [1984] make use of this metaphor). Religion is thought to perform a "priestly" function of legitimating political authority.[4]

In contrast, separatists have argued that the diversity of American religion makes religion a dangerous stranger to democratic discourse. Religious belief, it is argued, makes absolute truth claims that are not easily compromised by believers (Wald 1997). James Madison, in *Federalist #10* (perhaps the most widely cited of the *Federalist* papers), listed religion as a fertile source of "faction" and political instability (Hamilton et al. 1937). Indeed, many analysts have pointed to the sectarian violence taking place in other nations and contrasted it with the relative harmony among religions in the United States (Wayne 1995). Given the potential of religious difference as a source of political conflict, separatists tend to regard the purpose of the Establishment Clause as the depoliticization (or domestication) of religious belief through its confinement to a "private sphere" of activity (Levy 1986; Pfeffer 1967).

Religion is thought by some to be particularly dangerous to democratic politics, because religious commitments tend to be absolute and unadaptable to compromise. There is no guarantee that the sectarian violence that has characterized politics on the Indian subcontinent and in the Middle East, the Balkans, and Northern Ireland will not occur in the United States, as shown by the recurrent attacks on abortion providers (see Blanchard and Prewitt 1993; Blanchard 1994). A large literature in political science suggests that religious fervor is negatively related to support for essential democratic principles, such as freedom of speech and expression for nonconformists, and tolerance for diverse viewpoints (see Jelen and Wilcox 1990; Segers and Jelen 1998). In some instances, religion appears to have undermined the civility on which democratic politics arguably depends. For this reason, many separatists believe that a prominent public role for religion is incompatible with the practice of popular government in the United States.

In general, religious conflict is successfully managed in the United States (Wayne 1995). "Pro-life" violence is disturbing but rare and typically is denounced by mainstream abortion opponents (Maxwell 1995). Nevertheless, it is often suggested that such successful conflict management is a consequence of the depoliticized nature of American religion, which can perhaps be attributed to a fairly stringent interpretation of the Establishment Clause.

Separatists tend to interpret the Establishment Clause broadly, arguing that this portion of the First Amendment prohibits government assistance to religion in any form (Pfeffer 1967; Levy 1988). As Hugo Black stated in his opinion in *Everson v. Board of Education* (1947): "The 'establishment of religion' clause of the First Amendment means at least this: Neither a state nor the Federal government can set up a church. Neither can pass laws which aid one religion, *aid all religions*, or prefer one religion over another" (Cord 1982, 18 [emphasis added]). Thus, a separatist view of the Establishment Clause would prohibit even very general assistance to religion, even if such assistance was favored by a large majority of Americans.

Given this stance, it is not surprising that many accommodationists regard separatism as hostile to religion; indeed, one popular collection of accommodationist essays was titled *The Assault on Religion* (Kirk 1986). Yet although separatism might be consonant with opposition to religion, many separatists are deeply religious, and regard a strict boundary between the sacred and the secular as beneficial to both spheres.[5] A number of separatists have argued that the political role of religion is enhanced by strict independence from government assistance. In a religiously pluralistic society, religion is thought to fulfill the role of prophet/social critic, reminding political actors of standards emanating from a realm superior to that of secular politics (see Tinder 1989). This critical role might be compromised if religious bodies depended directly or indirectly on government support.[6]

Other religious supporters of separatism have voiced a different motivation: Roger Williams, a pastor in colonial Rhode Island, argued that the realms of religion and politics should be separated for the sake of religion, and not necessarily to preserve the essentials of democratic government. Williams regarded religion as a refuge from the corruption and debasement of worldly affairs, and suggested that clerical involvement in secular affairs would undermine the transcendence on which authentic religious belief ultimately depends (see Wills 1990; Segers and Jelen 1998).

A number of variations on the theme of religious freedom through independence are possible. It is quite possible to argue that religion is authentic only when freely chosen and freely formulated, and that state support might undermine that sort of religious freedom. Along these lines, an evangelical minister shared with me his reasons for opposing government assistance to parochial schools: "Once we take their money, sooner or later we'll have to accept their control. The price of [government assistance] is to have government coming in here, and telling us what we can or can't teach, or how we can discipline our children. . . . The price is just too darn high."

My conversation with an attorney at a recent conference of the American Bar Association ran in a similar vein. This particular lawyer had had extensive experience litigating church-state issues, and offered a highly theological rationale for a stance of religious separatism:

> You see, I believe in a literal Devil. Maybe not some cute little guy with horns and a pitchfork, but certainly a personal, supernatural being that represents the very embodiment of evil. I also believe that the Devil is capable of using the forms of religion to advance his aims, and that he does so quite frequently. As a lawyer and a citizen, I know that whatever rules are applied to one religion have to apply to all of them, whether they're true or false. So, whatever religious freedom might mean, I always think about whether I'd want to apply that standard to the Devil's church.

Thus, although it seems fair to assert that scholars who hold accommodationist views of the Establishment Clause have generally favorable views of the public effects of religion, the converse is not necessarily true. Although some separatists are clearly irreligious or antireligious, separatism as a constitutional principle is compatible with a number of different attitudes about the truth claims or social effects of religious belief and practice.

Similarly, one of two stances is generally adopted with respect to the Free Exercise Clause. A. James Reichley (1985) has identified these as **communalist** and **libertarian** understandings of religious free exercise. Adherents of both positions regard religious *beliefs* as inviolate; but communalists and libertarians differ on the extent to which religiously motivated *conduct* should be protected from government regulation.

Essentially, the communalist view of the Free Exercise Clause involves two assumptions: First, that the protection of religious free exercise means that religiously motivated groups can attempt to enact their policy preferences into law. That is, religious motivations are legitimate warrants or justifications for public policy positions (see Greenawalt 1988). This position, which is discussed in more detail in Chapter 4, reflects a strong sense of an important *public* role for religion. Second, religious *practices* can be regulated to the extent that they violate the moral or religious sensibilities of popular majorities as embodied in law. Actions that are otherwise illegal, in the communalist viewpoint, deserve no special protection because they are religiously motivated. The Free Exercise Clause simply means that government may not single out religious practices for special regulation.

To illustrate, consider the 1993 case of *Church of the Lukumi Babalu Aye v. City of Hialeah*. In this case, the U.S. Supreme Court struck down a municipal ordinance banning the Santerian use of animal sacrifice within the city of Hialeah, Florida. A communalist would support this reversal, since it seems clear that the regulation in question was directed at a specifically religious practice. However, a communalist would argue that if Hialeah had previously passed a more general measure banning the slaughter of animals within the city limits for any reason, such a ban would also apply to religiously based animal sacrifice. The Santerians' right of religious free exercise would not extend to an exemption from a more general restriction on certain uses of animals.

The communalist view of free exercise substantially qualifies the idea that free exercise is an inalienable right (Brisbin 1992). However, such a reading of the Free Exercise Clause is quite consistent with the majoritarian, consensual assumptions that underlie an accommodationist reading of the Establishment Clause. If one important purpose of religion is to promote an ethical consensus on fundamental rules of conduct, it follows that religious citizens who fall outside such a consensus will pose problems for the practice of democratic politics.

A libertarian view of free exercise, in contrast, entails the belief that with certain very narrow exceptions, religious practice should be exempt from government regulation. Unless government can show that a particular religious practice has immediate and severely harmful consequences (e.g., human sacrifice), a libertarian understanding of the Free Exercise Clause would allow religiously motivated exemptions from otherwise valid laws. In the animal sacrifice example cited above, libertarians would argue that the Santerians' right to practice their religion freely would supersede the city of Hialeah's right to restrict the killing of animals, regardless of the form of the particular city ordinance. Underlying the libertarian view of religious free exercise is the assumption that under most circumstances the requirements of citizenship may be trumped by particular religious or moral obligations. Religious belief and practice are thought to entail "higher" obligations that governments are bound to respect (see Carter 1993).

Questions of religious establishment and free exercise typically arise because modern government provides services that were not contemplated by the framers of the Constitution. In an era of activist government, the question is frequently posed as to whether the granting of a government service to religious groups equals unconstitutional "establishment," or whether the withholding of such services entails a restriction on the free exercise of religion. For example, consider the question of tuition tax credits granted to the parents of children attending private schools (an issue to which I return in the concluding chapter). Many separatists consider such credits a violation of the Establishment Clause, since religious schools—a large majority of private schools—indirectly benefit from them. Conversely, accommodationists might regard the denial of tuition tax credits as an infringement on the parents' right of religious free exercise, since without such credits, the parents of parochial school students would in effect be subjected to "dual taxation." That is, the parents of students at religious institutions pay taxes to support public schools (which their children do not use) and pay tuition at the private schools their children actually attend. Such a situation might be described as a violation of the Free Exercise Clause, since the taxation-plus-tuition burden renders the exercise of religious belief more costly. Clearly, this conflict between the Establishment and Free Exercise clauses would not exist if government were not in the business of providing public education.

A number of Free Exercise claims arise from the belief that government should exempt religiously motivated citizens from particular obligations. For example, during certain periods of American history, the U.S. government has conscripted young men for military service. In many such periods, the government has granted exemptions or substitute service for people whose religious convictions prohibited their participation in warfare. The existence of the legal classification of "conscientious objector" has typically been justified via reference to the Free Exercise Clause. Arguably, it is unjust (and unconstitutional) for government to require citizens to violate their religious beliefs. However, it has also been argued that making legal provision for conscientious objectors violates the Establishment Clause (see Choper 1995).[7] If religious denominations vary in the extent of their condemnation of warfare (as they clearly do) and if exemption from the risk of military service has value (as it clearly does), the government may well be discriminating in favor of traditional "peace churches" (e.g., Mennonites and Quakers) by allowing adherents of such denominations to avoid conscription. Indeed, access to the status of conscientious objector might be regarded as a government-created inducement to join particular churches, which would violate even a very narrow reading of the Establishment Clause.

In sum, the Establishment and the Free Exercise clauses coexist in a state of mutual tension. If government is active in promoting education, raising armies, and performing other social functions, then simple proscriptions against inter-ference or discrimination are inadequate guides for authorities' actions. To re-strict the scope of religious practice to the private sphere would seem to consti-tute a violation of the Free Exercise Clause, as the concept of religious free exercise might plausibly include attempts to embody religious values in public policy. However, any adoption or enforcement of religious values by government today would be commonly interpreted as a violation of the Establishment Clause.

The tension between the religion clauses of the First Amendment is typically noted more by separatists than by accommodationists. Accommodationists gen-erally argue that the Free Exercise and Establishment clauses are consistent and mutually supportive (see Monsma 1993; Monsma and Soper, 1997). However, such a reading is contingent on a particular narrow reading of the Establishment Clause and involves the prioritization of one clause over the other (Sherry 1992). Accommodationists generally would argue that the overall purpose of the religion clauses is to ensure religious liberty; and they would question any interpretation of the Establishment Clause that limited the prerogatives of religious individuals or organizations (Monsma and Soper 1997). In other words, for accommodation-ists, Free Exercise claims take priority over concerns about the unconstitutional establishment of state-sponsored religion.

Conversely, other scholars (Levy 1986, 1988) have echoed James Madison's ar-gument in *Federalist #10,* asserting that the religion clauses were intended to re-duce the potential for religious conflict by limiting the public presence of religion and confining religion to a private sphere of activity. Such a viewpoint is generally associated with an expansive reading of the Establishment Clause and would limit the application of the Free Exercise Clause to instances in which no issue of reli-gious establishment would likely be raised. As we will see in the next chapter, ef-forts to establish the "real" meaning of the religion clauses have resulted in little legal or scholarly consensus. Absent an authoritative definition of the concepts of religious free exercise and establishment, the tension between the two clauses seems likely to continue.

A Typology of Church-State Positions

The nature of the competing positions on the religion clauses of the First Amend-ment suggests that highly religious people can legitimately take a variety of stances on church-state relations. It is simply incorrect to regard accommodation-ism or libertarianism as "pro-religious," or separatism and communalism as the

FIGURE 1.1   A Typology of Church-State Relations

		Establishment Clause	
		Accommodationist	*Separationist*
	Communalist	Christian preferentialist	Religious minimalist
Free Exercise Clause			
	Libertarian	Religious nonpreferentialist	Religious free-marketeer

SOURCE: Ted G. Jelen and Clyde Wilcox, *Public Attitudes Toward Church and State* (Armonk, N.Y.: M. E. Sharpe, 1995), 25.

opposite. Moreover, there is no absolute correlation between positions on the Establishment and Free Exercise clauses.

Because there are several possible combinations of stances on the religion clauses, it is possible to construct a typology of possible church-state positions. This typology is displayed in Figure 1.1, where each cell represents the interaction between positions on religious establishment and free exercise.

Accommodationists (the first column) might take either libertarian or communalist positions on the Free Exercise Clause. Accommodationists who are also communalists (the upper left-hand quadrant) might be termed **Christian preferentialists**, because they would be likely to interpret the Establishment Clause broadly (permitting certain neutral types of government assistance to religion) and also would tend to restrict the free exercise prerogatives of groups falling outside a presumed cultural consensus. Persons in the quadrant might regard the United States as a Christian nation or believe that the United States should adhere to a Judeo-Christian tradition. Libertarian accommodationists (the lower left-hand quadrant) might be termed **religious nonpreferentialists**, since they might favor neutral government affirmation of religious values and tolerance of the free exercise claims of nonconventional religious groups.

Separatists who take a libertarian view of the Free Exercise Clause might be termed **religious free-marketeers**, since they might exhibit strong support for the free exercise claims of all religious groups but oppose government support for or affirmation of religion. Free marketeers might favor confining religion to a private sphere of activity but permitting maximum religious freedom within that sphere. Indeed, such people might be motivated as much by a desire to limit the activities of government in general as by attitudes toward religious issues. Finally, separatist communalists might be considered **religious minimalists**, since they apparently wish to minimize the role of religion in public life. Such people may wish to limit religious free exercise to majority groups, or to limit public support for religion. A minimalist position might entail the belief that religion deserves no special protection and that government should not support religious expression.[8] Although support for government *assistance* to religion is minimal within this category, minimalists predictably might allow government to enforce vigorously laws that proscribe harmful behavior, regardless of the presence of a religious motivation for violating such regulations.

Conclusion

The issue of church-state relations has an enduring presence in American politics. The importance Americans attach to religion, and the responsiveness of elected officials to public opinion, make it likely that policy questions involving the public role of religion will continue to figure prominently on the public agenda. Moreover, the separate yet overlapping jurisdictions of American political institutions have provided, and will likely continue to provide, potential for persistent conflict over this set of issues. The complex coexistence and interaction of various levels of government (federal, state, and local) and branches of government (executive, legislative, and judicial) have sustained a dynamic process in which religion can never truly be separated from questions of public policy.

Yet because church-state relations involve rights that the framers of the Constitution regarded as fundamental, citizens and their elected representatives play a necessarily limited role in determining the role of religious belief in public discourse and government policy; the central role is played by the judicial branch of government. Questions of religious freedom and religious autonomy from government are beyond the reach of the day-to-day operation of democratic politics, and for this reason, they constantly test the limits of governmental legitimacy. Because the Constitution provides ambiguous guidance concerning the proper role of religion in American politics, there is no scholarly, judicial, or popular consensus about the meaning of the concepts of religious establishment and free exercise.

Plan of the Book

The brief, almost abrupt language of the First Amendment has inspired many analysts to attempt to determine the historical origins and meaning of the religion clauses. In Chapter 2, I show how various historical analyses have animated contemporary discussions about the "authentic" meaning of the Establishment and Free Exercise clauses, and how history has become a contested rhetorical resource in modern religious politics.

In Chapter 3, I examine the different roles of the participants in the American political process with respect to church-state relations. The essential points in this chapter are the primacy of courts (especially the Supreme Court) in religious politics, and the effects of political decentralization on church-state questions. The separation of powers as well as the division of government authority among federal, state, and local jurisdictions have given many political leaders strong incentives to place church-state issues on the public agenda. Despite apparently definitive Supreme Court rulings, elected officials continually attempt to pass laws permitting organized prayer in public school, the teaching of creationism as science, the posting of the Ten Commandments in public school classrooms, and government support for religious schools. Chapter 3 explains why such a strategy may be advantageous for occupants of certain offices but not for others.

Chapter 4 addresses possible justifications for a strong presence of religion in American public life, and explores the arguments made by proponents of a prominent political role for religion. In Chapter 4, I argue that there has been a rhetorical shift in emphasis away from advancing religion as a source of social cohesion, and a corresponding increase in arguments promoting religion as a source of individual empowerment. Instead of describing religion as a set of restrictions on individual freedom, recent political arguments have suggested that religion is in fact an important source of political liberty. In constitutional terms, this involves a shift in political-ideological orientation from the Establishment Clause to the Free Exercise Clause.

In the final chapter, I offer an explanation of why religion continues to be such a vital issue in American politics at a time when it has disappeared from the agendas of most other Western industrialized nations. I suggest that this aspect of American exceptionalism has a firm basis in U.S. political institutions as a result of the interplay between American culture and the Constitutional regime. My argument rests on two fundamental factors: first, that the fragmenting tendencies of federalism and the separation of powers described in Chapter 3 have become stronger in recent decades and can be expected to continue to do so in the foreseeable future, reinforcing the current trend toward "public religion"; and second, that the Establishment Clause (which is unique to the United States) is a source of continuing legal tension (with the Free Exercise Clause), sustaining an environment within which high levels of religious belief and observance can flourish. That is, the same constitutional provision that limits the role of religion in American political life may be encouraging American citizens to promote religious values in the public sphere.

Questions for Discussion

1. Why should religion be regarded as a fundamental right? Does it make sense to regard religious freedom as an important individual prerogative? Why should government not discriminate among religions on the basis of the beliefs they espouse?

2. What should be the role of religion in politics? Is a genuine "separation" of church and state a viable option, or would such a separation violate the religious liberty of citizens?

3. What, if any, special legal rights should religious beliefs and practices have? Under what circumstances should government defer to the demands imposed on citizens by their religious beliefs? When is government regulation of religiously motivated behavior justified?

4. How are the four models of church-state relations presented in Figure 1.1 distinguished from one another? Which model most accurately describes contemporary church-state relations in the United States? Which would be most desirable?

Notes

1. This attempt was struck down as unconstitutional by a state court (*Las Vegas Review-Journal* 1999a).

2. In the U.S. judicial system, federal courts exist at three levels: At the lowest level are federal district courts, in which most federal cases originate. Rulings at this level can be appealed to one of eleven U.S. Courts of Appeals. Parties to court cases at the appellate level in turn can appeal verdicts to the U.S. Supreme Court. Most state court systems have a similar trilevel structure. However, less-populous states (such as Nevada) lack the intermediate appellate level. Appeals from the lower courts in these states are heard directly by the state supreme courts. Rulings from state supreme courts (known in legal parlance as "state courts of last resort") can be appealed directly to the U.S. Supreme Court.

3. See Tamney (forthcoming), Burns (1992), and Casanova (1994) for excellent discussions of this theme.

4. See Jelen (1991) and Leege and Kellstedt (1993) for discussions of this distinction.

5. See, for example, the accounts of the political thought of Roger Williams, James Madison, and Thomas Jefferson, in Wills (1990).

6. For example, some religious bodies risk losing their tax exemption if their political advocacy becomes too direct.

7. American citizens have no constitutionally protected *right* to religion-based exemptions from military service. The option of conscientious objection during periods of military conscription was created by Congress and presumably could be circumscribed or eliminated at Congress's discretion.

8. Several analysts (e.g., Casanova [1994]) have defined similar categories, some using the word *secularist* to describe the category I have called *religious minimalist*. I prefer *minimalist*, since no direct correlation has been established between the separatist-communalist position and hostility or indifference toward religion. On the contrary, empirical analysis suggests that many minimalists are religious, and reject a public role for religion primarily for theological reasons (see Jelen and Wilcox [1997]).

2

The Uses of History

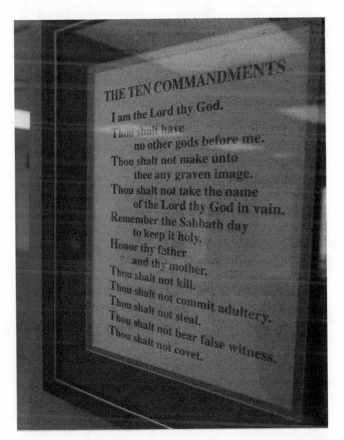

In recent years, a number of public school districts have posted the Ten Commandments in prominent places. The courts have declared this practice to be in violation of the Establishment Clause, since it seems to put a government agency (a public school) in the position of endorsing religion. However, school districts have continued in this practice. (AP/World Wide Photos)

・・・

In 1921, Supreme Court Justice Oliver Wendell Holmes observed that "a page of history is worth a volume of logic" (Driesbach 1997, 42). In perhaps no other area of American politics has this adage been applied more frequently and less productively than in church-state relations. Academic analysts and other protagonists in the ongoing controversy have made frequent use of historical arguments and evidence to bolster the case for their particular views of the Free Exercise and (most frequently) the Establishment clauses. However, this outpouring of scholarly and political rhetoric has not resulted in anything approaching a consensus on the "correct" use of history with regard to this set of issues. Rather, the historical record continues to provide ammunition for both separatists and accommodationists with respect to the Establishment Clause. In this chapter, I analyze the different interpretations attached to the history of the religion clauses of the First Amendment, attempting to account for the explosion of church-state controversies that occurred after World War II.

It is not my intention here to provide a detailed history of the adoption of the religion clauses of the First Amendment, nor a comprehensive account of the evolution of church-state law through the course of American history; such an undertaking is well beyond the scope of this volume. I would urge the reader to consult several other fine books in which this material is well covered (see, for example, Curry 1986; Cord 1982; Witte 1999; and Levy 1986 and 1988). My goal in this chapter is to provide an introductory guide to the historical controversies surrounding the First Amendment, conveying a sense of what is at stake with respect to particular claims about early American history; or in other words, to address the question "Who cares?"

Constitutional Heuristics

Implicit in any account of the history of church-state relations in the United States is the assumption that history matters. But why should our contemporary understandings of the proper role of religion in American politics depend in any way on the preferences and judgments of men long dead, whose values, circumstances, and contexts were vastly different from our own? Although the towering figures from America's colonial and revolutionary periods have become objects of veneration, it is not clear whether (or to what extent) we can ascertain their intentions; nor is it obvious that we should attempt do so.

The answer to this question lies in the role of **judicial review** in the American constitutional system. Religion is a constitutionally protected freedom; yet the Constitution provides ambiguous guidance to the makers of law and public policy regarding religion. Laws and policies with regard to the church therefore are frequently subject to legal dispute. Because governmental acts involving religious beliefs and organizations inevitably pose questions of a constitutional nature, the high courts—most visibly, the U.S. Supreme Court—play a central role in resolving legal questions arising from policymaking in this area. In deciding such matters, the courts rely on legal precedent—that is, on the record of judicial interpretations of previous, similar cases—as well as on the Constitution and the Bill of Rights.

Traditionally, in the Anglo-American system of jurisprudence—at least since the 1803 case of *Marbury v. Madison* (David and Brierly 1978)—the Supreme Court has had the power to invalidate laws passed by legislatures, if in the judgment of a majority of the Court's members such laws violate the U.S. Constitution. Judicial review is a blatantly undemocratic feature of the U.S. **separation of powers,** in that it places certain aspects of American public life, such as the proper functions of public authorities or the nature of individual rights, beyond the jurisdiction of elected officials, and by extension, outside the reach of popular majorities.

Some analysts, such as Edwin Meese (U.S. attorney general in the Reagan administration), have suggested that the power of judicial review should be modified or eliminated (Savage 1993). The Constitution itself makes no mention of judicial review. Most accounts of the origins of judicial review in the United States trace the concept to the Court's declaration of its own power in *Marbury.* For this reason, some recent commentators have suggested that the constitutional basis of judicial review is shaky. However, it seems clear that the power of judicial review is a settled feature of American jurisprudence. It is also evident that the Supreme Court's power of judicial review was intended by one or more of the framers of the Constitution. In *Federalist #78,* Alexander Hamilton stated:

> The complete independence of the courts of justice is peculiarly essential in a limited Constitution. . . . Limitations of this kind [abuses of legislative authority] can be preserved in no other way than through the medium of the courts of justice, *whose duty it must be to declare all acts contrary to the manifest tenor of the Constitution void.* Without this, all the reservations of particular rights or privileges would amount to nothing. (Hamilton et al. 1937, 505; emphasis added)

This passage suggests that some of the framers were suspicious of popularly elected legislatures and sought to limit the scope of legislative authority. Certain rights were intended to be beyond the reach of elected officials (and by extension, popular majorities), and the power of judicial review was regarded as an important safeguard against tyrannical or foolish majorities. Those who subscribe to the theory of **original intent** consider the Supreme Court's power to invalidate unconstitutional acts of popularly elected bodies an essential aspect of the separation of powers.

A full explication of the subject of judicial review is beyond the scope of this volume, but one aspect of the Court's power merits particular attention here. Since federal judges are not elected but are appointed for lifetime terms, they cannot be held accountable for their actions in the same manner as other public officials. Furthermore, the Supreme Court has the final word in legal disputes, and its decisions are not normally subject to review or appeal. This apparent lack of democratic accountability is perhaps the most controversial aspect of the Supreme Court's role in contemporary American politics. What, if anything, is to prevent the Court from acting as a sort of superlegislature, enacting its own preferences into law under the guise of constitutional interpretation?

Concerns about the effects of an unelected, unrepresentative judiciary have animated citizens at all points along the political spectrum. During the first half of the twentieth century, political liberals bemoaned the antidemocratic tendencies of the Supreme Court, as the Court struck down a number of legislative attempts to regulate health, safety, and child labor in the private sector, and later, as it invalidated many **New Deal** programs passed by Congress. Indeed, President Franklin Roosevelt was so frustrated by the Court's unwillingness to support the New Deal that he attempted a major reorganization of the Federal Courts in general, and the U.S. Supreme Court in particular (the so-called **court-packing** plan). Conversely, conservatives were most critical of the supposed **judicial activism** of the Supreme Court, as the **Warren Court** issued rulings requiring the desegregation of public schools, expanding the rights of those accused of criminal offenses, and prohibiting organized prayer in public schools. Since the Warren Court era, the **Burger** and **Rehnquist courts** have angered many religious conservatives by ruling that abortion is, under some circumstances, a constitutionally protected right, and extending the separatist tendencies of the Warren Court on church-state issues. The general point is that the Supreme Court has often invalidated highly popular acts of elected legislatures, and in the process, created and enforced extremely unpopular public policies.

Again, to assert that the power of judicial review is undemocratic is not to suggest that this prerogative of the courts is illegitimate. Indeed, implicit in the Constitution and the Bill of Rights is the assumption that certain governmental procedures, and certain human rights, are to be placed out of the reach of temporary majorities. The Constitution, and the Supreme Court's interpretation of the Constitution, is intended to protect the rights of minorities and to ensure the integrity of government lawmaking even when to do so is unpopular or inconvenient. However, the undemocratic nature of the system does create an obligation for justices to be particularly scrupulous when considering the reversal of decisions made by elected executives, legislators, and lower courts. Judicial review entails an assumption that judges will give priority to the Constitution over their personal preferences in deciding contemporary controversies and circumstances.

Given the essential importance of the Supreme Court's role in upholding the Constitution, it is often argued that a general principle of constitutional interpretation should be articulated and applied to judicial decisions. The Constitution, after all, is a brief, general document, full of broad phrases such as "necessary and proper," "cruel and unusual punishments," "due process of law," and "equal protection." The framers of the Constitution, as well as the authors of subsequent constitutional amendments, were attempting to create a document that would be applicable to a wide variety of unforeseeable circumstances, rather than one that would provide specific guidance in every imaginable instance. It is therefore not surprising that different observers, in sincere efforts to produce judgments that are in accordance with the principles of the Constitution, might apply these very general concepts in quite different ways. Without some sense of an agreed-upon method of constitutional interpretation and application, the Constitution risks becoming analogous to a psychologist's inkblot, with the meaning determined uniquely by each observer (see Bork 1990).

However, no such generally accepted interpretive method exists, or has ever existed. The nature of a proper "user's manual" for the U.S. Constitution has been the subject of frequent meta-analysis (see Tribe and Dorf 1991; Bork 1990), and frequent legal and academic controversy. One such proposed method, which has been particularly visible since early in the Reagan administration, is a jurisprudence of "original intent." Publicly advocated by former Attorney General Edwin Meese and defended by numerous conservative jurists and academics (see Bork 1990), the doctrine of originalism—or as Robert Bork has termed it, **interpretivism**—requires that in seeking the meaning of a particular constitutional provision, justices seek to understand the intentions of the authors of the document and to apply those intentions as faithfully as possible. To do otherwise, it is argued, risks substituting the justices' own subjective judgments for those of the framers (whose work has been legally ratified). Such "subjectivism," it is argued, would transform justices into unelected legislators.

Originalism or interpretivism is often contrasted with an approach that has been dubbed **evolving standards** (or more derisively, the "living Constitution" school; see Bork 1990 for a particularly scathing critique of this approach). The latter is often characterized (usually by originalists) as entailing the assumption that the Constitution must be continually reinterpreted to adapt to changing circumstances or contexts. However, relatively few constitutional scholars or justices have made explicitly revisionist arguments of an "evolving standards" type. Analysts on all sides of major constitutional issues have tended instead to invoke originalist arguments in support of their positions (see Dworkin 1997; Tribe 1997).

The idea that judicial activism is an illegitimate departure from a more structured, disciplined jurisprudence of originalism has become particularly salient in the past half century. The Supreme Court under Chief Justice Earl Warren (1953–1969) has often been described as a highly "activist" Court, in which the Constitution was interpreted very "creatively" and rights were established that are not necessarily explicit in the Constitution. Similarly, the Burger Court (1969–1986) has often been criticized by political conservatives and originalists for not reversing the activism of the Warren Court, and for extending the scope of certain constitutional protections (Savage 1993). Justice Burger's majority opinion in *Lemon v. Kurtzman* (1971)—the principal source of contemporary interpretations of the Establishment Clause—has been criticized by accommodationists for improperly limiting the ability of government to provide neutral assistance to religion. Despite the fact that the Burger Court contained four justices appointed by President Nixon (Warren Burger, Lewis Powell, Harry Blackmun, and William Rehnquist), the anticipated shift in American jurisprudence toward **strict constructionism** did not occur.

The principal intellectual issue dividing contemporary constitutional originalists from others involves the level of generality at which particular constitutional provisions are to be interpreted and applied. Recent analyses of constitutional interpretation have suggested that textual provisions are to be interpreted at the "most specific level at which a relevant tradition protecting or denying protection to the asserted right can be identified" (Scalia's concurring opinion in *Michael H. v. Gerald D.*, cited in Tribe and Dorf 1991, 73). Similarly, Bork (1990) has argued that one should consult the historical intentions of the framers to discern the appropriate level of generality at which constitutional provisions are to be interpreted. Thus, contemporary conservative jurisprudence suggests that constitutional provisions are to be read as narrowly as possible, to limit the possibilities for judicial lawmaking insofar as is practicable.

Examples may make this point clearer. In the case of *Griswold v. Connecticut* (1965), the Supreme Court struck down a Connecticut statute that prohibited artificial contraceptive devices. However, the Constitution establishes no explicit right to practice birth control. Writing for the Court's majority, Justice William O. Douglas located the right to use contraception within a broader, constitutionally based right to privacy—another right that is not explicitly mentioned in the Constitution. Douglas discovered (critics say he created) a right to privacy based on the **penumbra** of the Third, Fourth, and Fifth amendments to the Constitution. That is, underlying specific constitutional protections—such as those against quartering soldiers in peacetime (Amendment 3), unreasonable search and seizure (Amendment 4), and self-incrimination (Amendment 5)—Douglas perceived the existence of a zone of personal privacy or sovereignty with which government may not interfere. Although there is no specific mention of a right to privacy in the Constitution, the existence of such a right may arguably be inferred in the intentions of the framers.[1]

The existence of a constitutional right to privacy has been debated ever since *Griswold*. Conservative critics have argued that in *Griswold* the Court construed the Bill of Rights in an overly broad manner and in essence created new rights— rights neither foreseen nor endorsed by the framers of the Constitution. The right to privacy created in *Griswold* has since been extended to permit access to contraceptive devices among unmarried couples (*Eisenstadt v. Baird* [1972]); to bar states from prohibiting interracial marriage (the exquisitely titled *Loving v. Virginia* [1967]); and to allow abortion under certain circumstances (*Roe v. Wade* [1973]). More recently, however, the Court has declined to extend the right to privacy to consensual homosexual relations (*Bowers v. Hardwick* [1986]). Critics such as Robert Bork have argued that this entire line of cases, beginning with *Griswold*, represents a distortion of the Bill of Rights that has been compounded with each successive application of the *Griswold* precedent. From the standpoint of contemporary originalists, the mistake made in the Connecticut birth control case was methodological: The Court did not construe the Bill of Rights at the most specific level available, nor at a level that might have been endorsed by the First Congress, which passed the Bill of Rights. Put more simply, since the Constitution does not list a right to privacy (or for that matter, a right to birth control), it is illegitimate for anyone to assert that such *constitutional* rights exist.

In contrast, opponents of originalism have argued that the framers deliberately wrote the Constitution and the Bill of Rights in general language that could be adapted to a variety of changing and generally unforeseeable circumstances. The right to privacy asserted in *Griswold* was not created from whole cloth out of a judge's imagination; it is a legitimate extension of the intentions of the framers (see Tribe and Dorf 1991). One can hardly expect members of the Constitutional Convention or the First Congress of the United States to have anticipated developments in biotechnology, such as the availability of oral contraception. However, it is arguably unreasonable to suppose that no such prerogative can be afforded constitutional protection absent a specific provision in the Bill of Rights.

The quest for the appropriate level of specificity has been extended also to cases involving church-state relations. In 1994, in the case of *Board of Education of Kiryas Joel Village School District v. Grumet,* the Supreme Court ruled that the creation by the state of New York of a special school district for disabled children of Hasidic Jews (members of a highly orthodox, traditionalist branch of Judaism, in which believers are encouraged to live according to very precise biblical laws) was unconstitutional and a violation of the Establishment Clause (Biskupic 1994; Greenhouse 1994). In a sarcastic dissenting opinion, Justice Antonin Scalia wrote: "The Court today finds that the Powers that Be, up in Albany, have conspired to effect an establishment of Satmar Hasidim. . . . The Founding Fathers would be astonished to find that . . . the Court has abandoned text and history as guides. . . . Nothing prevents it from calling religious toleration the establishment of religion" (Greenhouse 1994, D22). Scalia argued that in order to support a violation of the Establishment Clause, the Court must prove that the state of New York had made Hasidic Judaism *the* established state religion. In an acid response, Justice David Souter made it clear that the majority's interpretation of the Establishment Clause was much broader than Scalia's historical construction: "The license he [Scalia] takes in suggesting that the Court holds the Satmar sect to be New York's established church is only one symptom of his inability to accept the fact that this Court has long held that the First Amendment reaches more than classic, 18th century establishments" (Greenhouse 1994, D21). Souter made clear his belief that although the *concept* of religious establishment has not changed since the days of the framers, the *application* of the Establishment Clause must be construed more broadly than was the practice two centuries ago. Souter argued that the Establishment Clause requires that "government should not prefer one religion over another, or religion to irreligion" (Greenhouse 1994, A1).

As these examples show, ascertaining the intentions of the framers of the First Amendment is an important legal and scholarly exercise to which enormous intellectual resources have been devoted. To the extent that one side of the separatist-accommodationist debate could present a credible description of the "original intent" of the "Founding Fathers" in support of a particular reading of the Establishment Clause, that side of the controversy would have an impressive rhetorical resource in the continuing controversy over church-state relations in the United States. However, careful examinations of the historical record have not resulted in anything approaching a consensus on the "authentic" meaning of the religion clauses of the First Amendment. Instead, a number of controversies con-

cerning historical evidence and interpretation have emerged. The next section
briefly surveys these controversies.

The Meanings of Religious Establishment

Until quite recently, most church-state litigation in the post–World War II era has
focused on the meaning of the Establishment Clause. The question of whether,
and under which circumstances, government may support, assist, or endorse religious practices and activities has been frequently disputed. For that reason, the
"correct" historical meaning of the Establishment Clause has been vigorously
contested by legal practitioners and scholars.

Historical Accommodationism

Many accommodationist analysts have suggested that the framers of the Constitution—especially the authors of the First Amendment—intended only a nonpreferentialist reading of the Establishment Clause. That is, the Establishment
Clause was *only* intended to proscribe the legal support of one particular church
by government, and any broader, more general reading of the Establishment
Clause distorts the historical record.

In support of a narrow, circumscribed reading of the Establishment Clause, a
number of arguments have been offered. First, it is often suggested that the
framers of the Constitution were religious men who had a keen appreciation of
the political importance of religious belief. For example, George Washington used
religious imagery to gain support for the American revolution, and favored
restoring an established church in Virginia in the subsequent decade. In retiring
from the presidency after his second term, Washington stated that "religion and
morality" were "indispensable supports" to political liberty. Washington argued
that "national morality" was unattainable without adherence to "a religious principle" (Reichley 1985, 102–103).

Accommodationist scholars have often suggested that religion was a priority
also among members of the founding generation whose beliefs were less orthodox or conventional than Washington's Anglicanism. James Madison, in opposition to an established church in Virginia, wrote as a Christian addressing other
Christians, and according to some analysts, argued that the principle of religious
toleration was a necessary consequence of Christianity. Madison suggested that
religious belief was a necessary component of good citizenship, and only voluntary adherence to Christianity could produce authentic faith and salvation

(Reichley 1985, 88). Even the author of the First Amendment, it has been argued, believed that there was an inseparable link between religious faith and responsible citizenship. Similarly, Benjamin Franklin, who is often characterized as a Deist, argued in favor of public religion as a component of public education in Pennsylvania, and regarded Christianity as preferable for this purpose to any other creed. Franklin believed that religion was a necessary aspect of the human personality, if citizens were to promote virtue and shun vice. No other means of restraining the natural tendencies of humankind would suffice (Reichley 1985, 101–102).

Perhaps most importantly, analysts of an accommodationist bent have suggested that Thomas Jefferson regarded religion as an essential component of a free society. The characterization of Jefferson as sympathetic to the public role of religion is important, since Jefferson is the source of many historical quotes cited by separatists to support their position.[2] For example, Jefferson is often quoted as saying: "It does me no injury for my neighbor to say there are twenty gods, or no God. It neither picks my pocket nor breaks my leg." As president, Jefferson wrote a letter to the Danbury Baptist Association in which he argued that the First Amendment erects "a wall of separation between church and state," which is among the most-quoted metaphors in American politics (Reichley 1985, 94). However, in drafting the Declaration of Independence, Jefferson also invoked God as the creator of natural and political rights ("all men are created equal, and are endowed by their creator with certain unalienable rights"). Jefferson argued on several other occasions that civil rights and liberties were a gift from God, and that there was no better basis for supporting political freedom (Reichley 1985, 95).

In this light, what are we to make of Jefferson's "wall" metaphor, or his celebrated agnosticism? One possible interpretation of Jefferson's thought is that he regarded the Establishment Clause primarily as a *jurisdictional* safeguard. That is, although religious establishment was an illegitimate activity on the part of the federal government, public support of religion (singular or plural) might still be an appropriate prerogative of state government (Driesbach 1997). Jefferson clearly did not favor any religious establishment in his home state of Virginia; but he appears to have regarded the abstract question of religious establishment as one that the state legislature was empowered to answer. Jefferson's oft-cited Virginia Statute of Religious Liberty (Segers and Jelen 1998, 130–131) is an act passed by an elected legislature, which Jefferson acknowledged could be (but should not be) overturned by subsequent assemblies. Although Jefferson regarded religious liberty as a natural right, he apparently believed that the right could be sufficiently protected at the state level by the normal political process of debate and compromise, and required constitutional protection only at the level of the (presumably remote) federal government.

In sum, accommodationists can point to a historical record showing that Jefferson and the framers of the Constitution were not hostile to religion, and in fact regarded religion as providing an important moral basis for citizenship. Although the specific beliefs of these people were heterodox in matters of doctrine, all regarded religion in general, and Christianity in particular, as constituting the basis of an ethical consensus without which popular government could not operate.

Second, it is often argued that the original purpose of religious disestablishment in colonial history, and in the early history of the American constitutional republic, was to protect religion from government, rather than vice versa. Indeed, Mary Segers (Segers and Jelen 1998) has shown that more than a century before the American Revolution, the metaphor of a "wall of separation" was used by Rhode Island minister Roger Williams. In the 1630s, the Rev. Williams had begun to practice in the Rhode Island colony, which was unusual in that it had no legally established church. However, Williams was no proponent of ecumenism, and indeed was quite critical of religions other than Puritanism, such as Quakerism, Anglicanism, and Catholicism (Wills 1990).

The metaphorical "wall" was intended to separate "the garden of the church from the wilderness of the world" (Segers and Jelen 1998, 72). For Williams, the purpose of church-state separation was to prevent the church from being contaminated by the corruption of secular politics. Secular authorities could be neither competent nor effective agents of religious conversion, and the very concept of a state religion was incompatible with Christian doctrine. Christianity was described by Williams and colonial dissenters as a religion of love, not of coercion, and they reiterated the belief that only voluntary adherence to Christianity could be regarded as the manifestation of authentic faith. A religious belief or practice that was not freely chosen would not, according to Williams, result in salvation for the compliant nonbeliever. Therefore, the institutional separation of church and state was intended to protect central religious values (in this case, individual salvation) rather than to serve specifically political ends.

Similarly, James Madison noted the negative effects of religious establishment on religious belief and practice, in his *Memorial and Remonstrance*, which was written in opposition to religious establishment in Virginia as engendering "pride and indolence in the clergy, ignorance and servility in the laity, . . . superstition, bigotry, and persecution" (Wills 1990, 376). Churches that received support from the government, Madison thought, lacked incentive to satisfy the spiritual and emotional needs of their congregations. Similarly, members of such established churches seemed likely to hold religious beliefs as a matter of convenience and social convention rather than as the result of conviction and faith. Thus, far from fearing the effects of religious involvement on secular government, Madison and Williams are often described as fearing the effects of government on religion.

Recent research in the sociology of religion has essentially supported the claims of Williams and Madison about the effects of religious establishment. A number of studies published in the 1990s suggest that religious observance and practice, as well as adherence to church doctrine, is more widespread and intense in settings in which a variety of faiths are practiced (see Iannaccone 1990; Finke and Stark 1992; and Jelen and Wilcox 1998). Where multiple denominations are forced to compete with one another, religious leaders must respond to the spiritual needs and demands of potential church members. In contrast, religious "monopolies" appear to have a depressive effect on church attendance and on public manifestations of religious belief.

The Williams/Madison argument about the religious basis for nonestablishment is thought to favor a nonpreferentialist position. Williams's notion of the "garden of the church," which requires protection from "the wilderness of society," is certainly not hostile to religion, and suggests that at least one purpose of disestablishment is the encouragement of authentic religious belief and practice. If the First Amendment was intended at least in part to promote religious faith, then it is difficult to argue that this constitutional provision should be interpreted to prohibit neutral governmental assistance to religion. Government support (direct or indirect) of multiple and competing denominations does not necessarily result in a religious monopoly or a loss of religious fervor.

Third, nonpreferentialist historians have attempted to show that the concept of religious establishment had a narrow, precise meaning in the late eighteenth century. As Gerard Bradley (1987, 3) put it: "Modern dictionaries define *establishment* as a state church, such as the Church of England or Church of Scotland. Traditional legal sources are in accord. Blackstone said that 'by establishment of religion is meant the setting up or recognition of a state church, or at least the conferring upon one church of special favors and advantages which are denied others.'"

Some accommodationist analysts have reached a similar conclusion on the basis of the historical record. For example, during congressional debates on the Bill of Rights, Madison said that the Establishment Clause only meant that "Congress should not establish a religion, and enforce the legal worship of it by law, or compel men to worship God in any manner contrary to their conscience" (Reichley 1985, 109; see also Cord 1982; Curry 1986; Driesbach 1997). In other words, the meaning attached to the concept of religious establishment when the First Amendment was written is arguably quite narrow: Such language refers to a specific, government-sponsored, religious-denominational monopoly. Religious establishments of this kind were fairly common in colonial America: Congregationalism was the established church in Massachusetts (and remained so for the first third of the nineteenth century), and Anglicanism (now called Episcopalianism) was the established church of Virginia. Thus, accommodationists have argued that the ban on religious establishment in the First Amendment was intended only to guarantee religious nonpreferentialism.

Indeed, in the Souter-Scalia exchange concerning the *Kiryas Joel* decision discussed earlier in this chapter, Souter implicitly accepts this version of history. In the majority opinion in *Kiryas Joel*, Justice Souter argues that his separatist ruling is a result of the fact that "the First Amendment reaches more than classic, 18th century establishments." Presumably, given this reading of the historical record, even a contemporary separatist like Souter would concede that if recent cases involving the Establishment Clause had been litigated during earlier periods of American history, some of the decisions reached would have been quite different.

Textual analysis of the Establishment Clause also has been used to support a nonpreferentialist reading of the First Amendment. As Michael Malbin (1978) pointed out, the Establishment Clause refers to *an* establishment of religion rather than *the* establishment of religion. Accommodationist scholars have taken the use of the article *an* to suggest that the Clause proscribes *particular* religious establishments but that a more general governmental assistance to religion is constitutionally permitted.

If a jurisprudence of original intent is the "correct" method of constitutional interpretation (as many conservative analysts have suggested), and if the authors of the First Amendment intended a narrow, nonpreferentialist reading of the Establishment Clause, contemporary separatist accounts of the First Amendment are incorrect. Language such as that used in *Everson v. Board of Education* (1947), in which Justice Black argued that the Establishment Clause proscribes "aiding all religions," is an illegitimate extension of the concept of religious establishment (see Driesbach 1997; Bradley 1987).

Fourth, it has been argued that the legislative history of the religion clauses of the First Amendment indicates that the original versions submitted to Congress contained explicitly nonpreferentialist language. The First Amendment, after all, was the result of a process of legislative deliberation, and therefore it should be possible to ascertain the intentions of the authors by examining the debates surrounding the adoption of the religion clauses during the First Congress. The spare language of the First Amendment often seems frustratingly imprecise; but we can perhaps enhance our understanding by consulting the records of the deliberations surrounding the adoption of the religion clauses. Such a historical examination could provide the intellectual context in which the meaning of the First Amendment was formulated.

Several analysts have attempted to demonstrate that congressional debate on the First Amendment had a clear, nonpreferentialist focus. For example, one of Madison's early formulations of the Establishment Clause simply proscribed the creation of a "national religion" (Cord 1982; Bradley 1987). Madison withdrew this version when discussion focused on the proper scope of federal authority with regard to religion, because a proscription against a "national religion" carried the clear implication that the Constitution had created a national government (a sore point that had to be finessed in order to achieve ratification of the First Amendment). Madison's draft amendment read: "The civil rights of none shall be abridged on account of religious belief or worship, nor shall any national religion be established, nor shall the full and equal rights of conscience be in any manner, or any pretext, abridged" (Reichley 1985, 108). A revised House version read, "No religion shall be established by law, nor shall the equal rights of conscience be infringed" (ibid., 109). Still another version, proposed by Rep. Samuel Livermore of New Hampshire, read, "Congress shall make no laws touching religion, or infringing on the rights of conscience" (Levy 1988, 180). The explicit limitation on the powers of Congress made clear that the Amendment was not intended to interfere with existing state establishments, and allowed legislators to avoid the touchy subject of the distribution of authority between federal and state governments.

The historical record shows that in the congressional debate over religious establishment, multiple goals and issues were being contested. The specific language of the First Amendment, like that of any other legislative enactment, was the result of compromises between officials with different and often conflicting motives. However, accommodationists wish to make clear that there was no specific disagreement in the House debates on the Establishment Clause respecting the scope of the First Amendment. It is argued by scholars from this perspective that the First Amendment (indeed, the entire Bill of Rights) was intended simply to limit the power of the *federal* government to endorse or support a *particular* religion.

Fifth, many accommodationists argue that early presidents, such as Madison and Jefferson, executed official acts that can only be characterized as accommodationist. In such historical analyses, it is particularly instructive to examine the official acts of President Madison, who played an important role in the writing of the Constitution and in the legislative debates over the Bill of Rights, and of President Jefferson, whose writings are the source of much historical separatist rhetoric (including the oft-quoted "wall of separation" metaphor). It seems clear that both

Madison and Jefferson often acted in a manner designed to accommodate public acknowledgments of religious values. Jefferson (clearly the more separatist of the two) discontinued the practice of Federalist Presidents Washington and Adams of proclaiming national days of thanksgiving, on which citizens were encouraged to thank the Creator for His blessings. However, Jefferson consistently provided government funding for Catholic missionaries to minister to Native American tribes (Cord 1982; Bradley 1987). Madison continued this practice, and also revived the Washington-Adams habit of declaring national days of thanksgiving. Thus, accommodationists have argued that members of the founding generation who were most conspicuously positioned to implement the provisions of the new Constitution apparently held a narrow, nonpreferentialist understanding of the religion clauses of the First Amendment.

What all this suggests, of course, is that accommodationist historians and political scientists have gone to great lengths to expose and illuminate a historical record that suggests the importance of religious free exercise (hence, their frequent appeals to "the rights of conscience") and a correspondingly narrow view of the Establishment Clause. Government (in this instance meaning *only* the federal government) was proscribed from favoring *a* religion but was not legally prevented from encouraging the practice of religion in general.

Historical Separatism

Separatists have derived a broader, more general reading of the Establishment Clause from the same historical record. Their analyses suggest that a nonpreferentialist reading of the Establishment Clause is much too narrow an interpretation, and that even nondiscriminatory government assistance to religion is inconsistent with the intentions of the Constitution's framers.

Separatist historians such as Leonard Levy (1986, 1988) have argued that the meaning of religious establishment was by no means as settled as nonpreferentialists have suggested. During the colonial period, several colonies had extensive experience with various forms of **multiple establishment**. In states such as New York and New Hampshire, a sort of "home rule" religious establishment prevailed. That is, individual communities were free to provide government support for one or several churches, to be selected locally. Indeed, Levy (1988, 186) reports that the English government had mandated the establishment of Anglicanism during the colonial period of New York history, but the colonial legislature defied the British by mandating a more general system of religious establishment. New York in the mid–seventeenth century required local governmental support for a "good and sufficient Protestant minister." Even in Massachusetts, in which Congregationalism was legally established as the official state religion, towns dominated by other denominations legally established local churches of their own denomination. Further, it has also been shown (Levy 1986) that a number of newspapers in New England were quite critical of a decision on the part of the Canadian government to support both Anglicanism and Roman Catholicism, because such action "established Romanism" (a very unpopular creed in colonial New England).

Thus, the practice of multiple religious establishment was arguably familiar to politically active citizens around the time of the founding of the Bill of Rights, and the Establishment Clause can plausibly be read to proscribe this more general form of governmental support. If such an analysis is correct, the clear implication is that the framers' use of the phrase *establishment of religion* has a broader scope than classical, European establishments of a single, state-supported church. To the extent that religious establishment is a proscribed practice at a particular level of government (an issue to be discussed below), separatists would hold that the prohibition applies to general, as well as specific, establishments of religion.

Separatists assert that the legislative intent of the First Congress is by no means as clear as accommodationist historians have suggested. Although the debate on the religion clauses in the House of Representatives makes clear that many House members clearly intended only nonpreferentialism, the records of the first U.S. Senate also make it clear that the Senate explicitly rejected three nonpreferentialist versions of the Establishment Clause. On the same day, the U.S. Senate defeated three motions that employed nonpreferentialist language: One of these prohibited Congress from establishing "one religious sect or society in preference to another"; a second proscribed the establishment of "any religious sect or society"; and a third forbade Congress to establish "any particular denomination of religion in preference to another" (Levy 1988, 181). If legislative action is the best available indication of the intent of a legislative body, separatist historians have argued, the historical record shows that the first U.S. Congress, both House and Senate, rejected the accommodationists' preferred interpretation of the First Amendment.

Some separatists have also gone into fine detail examining the language of the First Amendment. Levy (1986) argues that the Establishment Clause does not simply proscribe legal religious establishments but enjoins Congress from passing *any* law respecting an establishment of religion. Rather than simply prohibiting one particular sort of legal arrangement, Congress is forbidden to address the topic altogether. As we will see later in this chapter, this limitation on the powers of Congress has subsequently been applied to state and local governments as well.

A comparable analysis is possible with respect to the Free Exercise Clause. Note that the First Amendment bars Congress from making laws *prohibiting* the free exercise of religion but *abridging* the rights of free speech and free press. If one interprets these two verbs literally, as those who favor "strict construction" of the Constitution suggest (Scalia 1997), it might well be argued that the rights of freedom of speech and press were more carefully protected by the framers than was the right of religious free exercise, since government is presumably permitted to make laws abridging but not prohibiting the free exercise of religion (Levy 1986). If such a reading of the First Amendment is in fact justified, this makes the accommodationist claim that the Free Exercise Clause ought to have priority over the Establishment Clause appear rather implausible. A narrow, constructionist interpretation of the Free Exercise Clause could plausibly assert that government (including Congress) has broad powers to regulate religious free exercise, short of outright prohibition.

Support for such an assumption is found in the fact that James Madison later recanted the accommodationist acts passed during his presidency. Both accommodationists and separatists appear to agree that because he was the "father of the Constitution," Madison's views should be given great weight in any assessment of the original intent of the "Founding Fathers." In his *Detached Memorandum*, written in retirement in 1817, Madison expressed regret for having engaged in the accommodationist practice of proclaiming national days of thanksgiving and observed that governmentally supported religious observances were "probably unconstitutional" (Levy 1986; Fleet 1946). In this final work, Madison also decried the accumulation of untaxed church wealth, tax-supported chaplains, and the increased public power and prestige of the clergy (Wills 1990, 374). On the basis of these writings, some separatists argue that Madison changed his mind about the "correct" meaning of the Establishment Clause. The idea seems plausible when we consider that Madison, as a member of the first U.S. Congress and later as president, was privy to the internal functioning of the new, untested set of institutions, and that some later reassessment may have been inevitable. In any event, Madison's last word on the subject of church-state relations appears to have been explicitly separatist.

Levy (1986) has argued that a nonpreferentialist reading of the Establishment Clause is inconsistent with the purpose of the Bill of Rights. If the Constitution confers on the federal government only a set of *enumerated* powers, it has only those powers explicitly granted to it. This assumption is made explicit in the **Tenth Amendment**, which grants all powers not expressly conferred on the federal government by the Constitution to the states, or to the people. Since the federal government was not explicitly given any powers in the area of religion, it must be inferred that it has none. If the Establishment Clause is read as having a nonpreferentialist meaning, then the clause effectively creates a positive power for the federal government. If nonpreferentialism means anything at all, it means that government is permitted to provide neutral, nondiscriminatory assistance to religion and that the Establishment Clause *only* proscribes favoring one religion over another. If this reading is correct, the First Amendment would have the effect of empowering government to provide neutral support for religion. Levy (1986) argues that such an interpretation is entirely inconsistent with the clear purpose of the Bill of Rights. The first ten amendments to the U.S. Constitution impose *limitations* on the power of government, and a set of citizen rights with respect to government. It seems implausible to assert that, uniquely among the provisions of the Bill of Rights, the Establishment Clause increases the power of the federal government. An accommodationist reading of the First Amendment arguably contradicts the spirit of the Bill of Rights—that is, the limitation of powers.[3]

Even if a nonpreferentialist reading of the Establishment Clause were the correct historical understanding, it does not follow that the application of this principle cannot change, or has not changed, in the two centuries since the First Congress convened. The application of the principle might vary enormously, depending on the extent of religious diversity. The concept of "neutrality" can be assigned specific meaning only in particular contexts. That is, government can only act "neutrally" *among* a set of alternatives. If the nature of the alternatives changes, so might the application of the principle of nonpreferentialism.

For example, an organized prayer in a public school that makes specific reference to the divinity of Jesus Christ might well be considered neutral in a student body that consists entirely of Protestants and Catholics. Since Christ's divine nature is not typically contested among Christians (indeed, it might be argued that such a belief is a defining characteristic of Christianity), such a prayer might legitimately be considered nondiscriminatory and thus permissible under an accommodationist understanding of the First Amendment. However, it seems reasonable to suppose that such "neutrality" would be shattered if the prayer were imposed on a student body that contained Jews, Muslims, or Hindus. Similarly, a prayer addressed to "Almighty God" might appear neutral to a group of Christians and Jews but would seem discriminatory if the group in question included (polytheistic) Hindus.

Even if it is conceded that the First Amendment does not require neutrality between religion and irreligion and that atheists have no rights under the Establishment Clause (which is an *extremely* implausible assumption), the presence and increased visibility of non-European immigrants makes authentic religious neutrality increasingly problematic. As we will observe in the following chapter, members of the mass public who hold accommodationist viewpoints often come to see the merits of separatism when presented with the possible necessity of ac-

commodating Buddhism, Hinduism, or Islam. If the principle of religious neutrality is extended to include such "cults" as Hare Krishnas, followers of the Rev.
Sun Yong Moon, or Scientologists, it might be anticipated that the willingness of a
majority to accommodate religion "in general" might be more limited still (see
Jelen and Wilcox 1995). If we recall the remarks of the attorney quoted in Chapter
1, who was concerned about the rights that might be extended to the "Devil's
church," the possible limits of nonpreferentialism might seem even more compelling to accommodationists.

In sum, the extensive literature written in an attempt to explain the intentions
of the "Founding Fathers" with respect to questions of religious freedom and establishment has generated much more heat than light. If intellectual progress is
signaled by increasing consensus among sophisticated analysts, then it must be
conceded that not much progress has been made in the historical exegesis regarding the authentic meaning of the religion clauses of the First Amendment.

Constitutional Tie-Breakers

Even conceding that the historical record of the intentions of the framers is not
particularly helpful, accommodationists and separatists have markedly different
senses of which institutions should resolve apparent conflicts over the meaning of
the religion clauses. Because accommodationists have tended to emphasize the integrative, consensual role of religion in American politics, enacting the public's
will on matters of church-state relations is generally perceived as beneficial.
Judges, lacking such accountability, do not have so simple a means of rectifying
errors in constitutional interpretation, and should therefore defer to the more
democratic branch of government in situations where the meaning of the Constitution is unclear. As Justice Bork has written, "There being nothing to work with,
the judge should refrain from working" (Bork 1990, 166). For judges to substitute
their will for that of the majority is, from an accommodationist standpoint, to
subvert the democratic process.

Separatists, in contrast, have tended to emphasize the potential for conflict in
the public expression of religious belief, and have thus been less sanguine about
the wisdom of the people, and by extension, of the people's representatives. The
problem of the "tyranny of the majority" (Tocqueville 1945) is a constant concern
of those who favor minimizing the role of religion in public life. Implicit in the
very concept of a "right" is the notion that rights are prerogatives that lie beyond
the reach of popular majorities. Thus, the "right" not to be subjected to religious
establishment, or to religious free exercise, should not depend on the prevailing
winds of popular sentiment. Judges, if removed from direct accountability to

public opinion, are in a much better position than elected officials to protect the rights of unpopular religious minorities.

The Postwar Explosion

It is perhaps of some interest that the religion clauses of the First Amendment did not occasion much in the way of political conflict prior to World War II. Indeed, for the first 150 years of the Constitution's existence, only one major religion case was litigated before the Supreme Court. The 1879 case of *Reynolds v. U.S.* concerned the Mormon practice of polygamy. The Court decided that the Free Exercise Clause did not proscribe government prohibition of the practice. A few cases involving the religion clauses of the First Amendment were decided in the early 1940s *(Cantwell v. Connecticut; Minersville School District v. Gobitis; West Virginia State Board of Education v. Barnette).* The constitutional conflict concerning the appropriate public role of religion in such matters virtually exploded during the period following World War II (Robbins 1993).

There appear to be four principal reasons for the postwar explosion in church-state litigation. First, the population of the United States in the second half of the twentieth century has been characterized by much greater religious diversity than had previously been the case. The United States has been a primarily Protestant nation for most of its history (Cord 1982), with several waves of Catholic and Jewish immigration in the period following the American Civil War. More recently, non-European immigrants have become more visible in American society, and many of these people practice religions outside the Judeo-Christian tradition. In addition, new religious groups (including those characterized as "cults") have achieved a high level of visibility in contemporary American politics. Groups such as the Hare Krishnas (the bane of air travelers throughout the United States), so-called "Moonies," and Satanists are regarded by many in the United States as lying outside the range of religious respectability.

This increase in religious diversity has had at least two important consequences. First, the increased religious visibility of those outside the Judeo-Christian tradition has often led to increased attempts at government regulation of religious practice. Many Americans are reluctant to extend religious liberty to those whose beliefs and practices are regarded as strange or dangerous (Jelen and Wilcox 1995). This in turn has meant that there has been no shortage of potential plaintiffs in cases involving the Free Exercise Clause. Practitioners of unpopular religions have often resisted attempts by government to regulate their religious practices. For example, in the 1993 case of *Church of the Lukumi Babalu Aye v.*

City of Hialeah, the Court struck down a local ordinance banning animal sacrifice within the city limits. Obviously, the occurrence of such a ruling depends on the existence and enforcement of a law banning this unconventional religious practice, and a group willing to violate such a law. Such an issue is unlikely to come up in a jurisdiction containing only Catholics, Methodists, and Presbyterians. Second, adherents of unconventional religions are also likely plaintiffs in cases involving the Establishment Clause. What might appear to be religiously "neutral" within a relatively narrow range of religious beliefs may appear to be biased when presented to a religiously more diverse population. For example, a "nondenominational" prayer addressed to "Almighty God" may be inoffensive to a group comprised of Christians and Jews, but offensive to Muslims (who may object to the omission of the name "Allah") or Hindus (whose theology is polytheist). If the audience for a public gathering (such as a classroom, a graduation ceremony, or sporting event) contains persons whose religious heritage is non-European, a public ritual that formerly appeared innocuous may become the occasion for political conflict or litigation.

The increasing religious diversity of the United States is a primary source of political and legal conflict, since constitutional principles are not typically self-executing: Even if the right of religious free exercise or the proscription of religious establishment has been violated, some person or group must file suit before the U.S. courts will act. The large numbers of religious minorities in contemporary American society mean that potential plaintiffs are much more available.

Religious conflict became more frequent and more intense in the post–World War II era also because government at all levels began to offer more services, and increased the taxes it collected to pay for those services. Citizens living in the United States since the New Deal of the 1930s, and even moreso since the **Great Society** of the 1960s, are likely to have a good deal more interaction with government than had previous generations. Health care, transportation, retirement benefits, scholarships, and other government activities render contact between citizens and government at various levels more frequent and potentially more intrusive. Such increased contact with government greatly expands the potential for conflicts over church-state relations. For example, if a Catholic hospital were denied government grants because the administrators refused to allow abortions to be performed in that facility, would the withholding of the government subsidy be an unconstitutional restriction on the free exercise of religion? Has government not rendered the application of Catholic doctrine more costly by refusing funding available to other hospitals? Conversely, would the provision of such grants amount to an unconstitutional "establishment" of Catholicism (Labi 1999)? This sort of problem is often quite difficult to resolve. What seems clear, however, is that the issue is unlikely to be raised in contexts in which the provision of health care is confined to the private sector of the economy. This point can be generalized: In the post–New Deal era, the U.S. government has assumed at least partial responsibility for a variety of functions and services that traditionally were outside its legitimate jurisdiction. Moreover, services such as health care, education, and assistance to the poor have long been regarded as important tasks of religious organizations. To the extent that the tasks of government and religion overlap, the constitutional issues raised by church-state separation will be encountered much more frequently.

A third important factor in the increased frequency of church-state conflict was the "Warren Court" (named after Chief Justice Earl Warren, who served from 1953 through 1969), which ushered in an era of judicial activism. With a greater potential for access to the high courts, interest groups have more frequently resorted to litigation to forward their agendas. Arguably, since the landmark case of *Brown v. Board of Education of Topeka* (1954), the Supreme Court has shown an increased willingness to issue rulings that have extraordinarily broad implications for politics and society; and some individuals and groups have sought to take advantage of this tendency by having their grievances addressed by the federal courts. This strategy is particularly likely to succeed if the group in question is a small and perhaps relatively unpopular minority, which is often the case in cases involving the religion clauses of the First Amendment.

In cases involving alleged violations of the Establishment Clause, plaintiffs are typically citizens outside the religious mainstream in a particular context or jurisdiction. As we will see in the next chapter, most citizens do not see any problem with certain public assertions of religious beliefs or practices, and it often falls to members of minority religions or atheists to point out possible constitutional violations. Such minority-supported challenges to prevailing local practices are by definition unpopular, and are therefore unlikely to be raised by elected officials. For example, in a community whose population is predominantly Christian, a majority may see no problem with placing a Nativity scene at the city hall during December. It is often someone who does not share the religious commitments of the community's majority—a Jew, a Muslim, or a person without religious affiliation—who objects to the public display of religious sentiments.

Similarly, in cases involving alleged unconstitutional restrictions on religious free exercise, citizens with grievances are most likely to be members of unconventional and unpopular religions, whose practices elected officials often seek to restrict. Thus, free exercise issues are often raised over the rights of religious groups to use hallucinogenic drugs, to engage in animal sacrifice, to practice polygamy, or to engage in aggressive (and usually annoying) religious propaganda in public places. Almost anyone who has been accosted by a "Moonie" or Hare Krishna in an airport or shopping mall can understand the popularity of measures designed to restrict such activity, and by extension, the desire of elected legislators and executives to use such feelings to political advantage. Candidates for election often have quite reasonable fears about being labeled "pro-drug," "pro-cult," or "pro-Moonie," and it may not be reasonable to expect candidates to place a high value on protecting the rights of religiously defined marginal citizens. In either case, the sense of marginality experienced by religious minorities has made them more willing to adopt a strategy of litigation to redress their grievances of religious discrimination or unconstitutional religious establishment (see Way and Burt 1983). The assertion of unalienable "rights" by members of minority groups is in fact undemocratic (if perhaps desirable on other grounds), and therefore may be best protected by members of an unelected judiciary.

Lastly, church-state conflict increased in the post–World War II era in part as a response to the doctrine of **incorporation** (Levy 1986, 1988; Friendly and Elliot 1984). If one reads the First Amendment literally, the prohibitions against restrictions on freedom of speech, religion, press, and assembly are directed at *Congress*, and not at state or local governments. Indeed, the Tenth Amendment, which guarantees that powers not specifically attributed to the federal government are retained by the states and the people, is often thought to reinforce the notion that the entire Bill of Rights is a set of restrictions on the federal government and does not apply to subnational jurisdictions. In the case of the religion clauses, as noted earlier in this chapter, some form of state religious establishment was a common feature of state government at the time the Constitution was enacted, and such state religious establishments continued to exist for the first third of the nineteenth century (Levy 1988; Cord 1982).

Since the end of the Civil War, the distinction between federal and state governments as settings in which the Bill of Rights should be applied has eroded steadily. In most (but not all) instances, citizens of the United States now enjoy the same legal protections at all levels of government. Gradually, through a long sequence of Court decisions, the Bill of Rights has been "incorporated" to include state and local governments. This process began in 1897, in the case of *Chicago, Burlington, and Quincy Railroad Co. v. Chicago*, and steadily expanded to include several of the first ten amendments to the Constitution (McDowell 1993).

The doctrine of incorporation has its constitutional basis in the **Due Process Clause** of the Fourteenth Amendment, which was ratified in 1868. The clause reads, "Nor shall any State deprive any person of life, liberty, or property without due process of law." The current consensus on the meaning of this phrase—which has evolved through accumulated judicial interpretations—is that the Fourteenth

Amendment created a form of national citizenship, and that the Bill of Rights therefore applies to all levels of government (see Kluger 1977 for an account of how this amendment came to be applied to state governments through a series of cases of racial discrimination).[4] The religion clauses were first applied to actions of state and local governments in the 1940s. In *Cantwell v. Connecticut* (1940) and the more famous (or infamous) 1947 case of *Everson v. Board of Education* (see Formicola and Morken 1997), the courts held that the Establishment and Free Exercise clauses limit the actions of state governments as well as those of the federal government. However, the process of incorporation was gradual, and proceeded on a number of different constitutional tracks. For example, the "exclusionary rule" that prohibits the use of illegally obtained evidence in criminal trials was first applied to federal courts in the 1914 case of *Weeks v. United States,* and criminal defendants did not hold similar rights in state courts until *Mapp v. Ohio* (1961).

Because of the gradual nature of the process, the doctrine of incorporation has been quite controversial. The scope of the Fourteenth Amendment has been contested with particular intensity when the religion clauses of the First Amendment have been at issue (Kirk 1986; Driesbach 1997). For example, the issue of the extent of the Fourteenth Amendment was a prominent issue in the Alabama gubernatorial election of 1998, as Republican candidate Fob James made the assertion of Christian symbols in public life the centerpiece of his campaign. James argued that restrictions on practices such as organized prayer in public schools (or at high school football games), or the display of the Ten Commandments in public schools were based on the Supreme Court's misreading of the Due Process Clause (Johnson 1999).[5] In a more scholarly but no less spirited argument, A. James Reichley (1985) has suggested that the Fourteenth Amendment can be applied legitimately to the Free Exercise Clause, because religious free exercise is a protected liberty under the Due Process Clause. However, Reichley argues that it is incorrect to apply the Establishment Clause to the actions of state or local governments, since no protected liberty is at stake. In this analysis, then, citizens are entitled to protection from infringements on their religious liberty by state governments, but enjoy no similar constitutional protection against state religious establishments.

In sum, the incorporation of the Bill of Rights to apply to state governments is a well-established but by no means settled principle of constitutional interpretation. The precise reach of the Fourteenth Amendment is of extreme importance in the resolution of church-state issues, because an overwhelming percentage of such cases are initiated at the state and local levels, in response to the actions of subnational governments. Indeed, many church-state controversies involve issues of public education. Mandatory observance of the Pledge of Allegiance, organized school prayer, the observance of religious holidays by public schools, and the teaching of **scientific creationism** all involve the actions of local teachers, principals, and school boards. Similarly, issues of the enforcement of Sabbath laws and religious displays in public places are more often than not contested at the local level. To the extent that incorporation is a standard feature of constitutional interpretation in the future, it seems likely that church-state litigation will continue to occupy a prominent place on the dockets of American courts.

Conclusion

The dilemma of church-state relations has at least two important historical dimensions. First, the interpretation of the intentions of the framers of the First Amendment is vigorously contested by both academic and legal analysts of the political role of religion. Both sides of the church-state debate have sought to control the meaning of history, which has rendered the controversy extremely intense during the last generation or so. Indeed, it seems likely that the importance attached to these issues has made their resolution more difficult.

Second, the intensity of the debate over "original intent" has increased since World War II. A number of trends in American social and political life have given the issue of church-state relations, which generally had lain dormant for the first 150 years of American history, a central place on the contemporary political agenda. Changes in the general style of constitutional interpretation, the role of government in society, and the religious composition of the population all have contributed to the increased salience of church-state issues in the routine operation of American politics. In the next chapter, I survey the practice of religious politics in the United States today.

Questions for Discussion

1. Is it possible for people living in the twenty-first century to understand the intentions of people who lived in the eighteenth? Assuming it is possible, what weight should be given to the beliefs and values of people long dead? If such understanding is not possible, on what might people base their interpretation of constitutional provisions?

2. What is the appropriate level of generality at which provisions of the Constitution (such as the Bill of Rights) should be interpreted? What risks are involved in employing various levels of constitutional interpretation?

3. Is the application of the Bill of Rights to state and local governments a legitimate extension of constitutional provisions? Has "incorporation" subverted or undermined the powers of subnational governments?

Notes

1. Such inferences are generally warranted by reference to the Ninth Amendment, which states, "The enumeration in the Constitution, of certain rights, shall not be construed to deny or disparage others retained by the people." Thus, the Bill of Rights, as well as subsequent amendments, is not to be considered an exhaustive list of rights held by U.S. citizens. In his concurrence in *Griswold,* Justice Arthur Goldberg relied heavily on the Ninth Amendment, which he argued licenses the search for a "right to privacy." For a more limited view of the Ninth Amendment, see Bork 1990.

2. Jefferson was not, strictly speaking, a "founding father" of the Constitution, although he was the author of the Declaration of Independence. He was representing the newly independent states in France at the time of the writing of the Constitution, in 1787.

3. However, arguments invoking the "spirit" of the Bill of Rights typically violate originalists' demand for specificity. A constructionist interpretation of the Constitution also would require considerable skepticism about an argument invoking the "entire purpose" of the first ten amendments.

4. The constitutional interpretation of the Fourteenth Amendment has been complicated by the Court's very narrow interpretation of the "privileges and immunities" clause of the amendment in the *Slaughterhouse Cases* in 1872. The clause reads: "No state shall make or enforce any law which shall abridge the privileges and immunities of citizens of the United States." Although the clause could be interpreted as a straightforward justification for the incorporation of the Bill of Rights to include state governments, the Court in 1872 chose to assign it a more limited meaning. Subsequent courts have honored the *Slaughterhouse* precedents, justifying the doctrine by reference to the due process clause. For a more complete account, see Sezer 1995.

5. Although James was victorious in the GOP primary, he was defeated in the general election.

3

Debating the Public Role of Religion

The Protagonists

In the United States, religious liberty is claimed by adherents of a wide range of beliefs. Here, a Santerian displays an eclectic collection of religious symbols. (Photo © Tony Arruza/CORBIS)

In a democratic republic, it is expected that there will be at least an approximate correspondence between public opinion and public policy. Nevertheless, because the framers of the U.S. constitutional system were suspicious of the influence of the mass public, they interposed numerous obstacles between public sentiments and the making of the laws. The separation of governmental powers at the federal level, and the distribution of powers among different levels of government in an arrangement called *federalism,* have provided activists in the politics of church-state relations various access points to political decisionmaking. Citizens interested in the politics of religion have many opportunities to make their voices heard. Perhaps paradoxically, the same characteristics of U.S. politics have made the issues involved in church-state relations difficult to resolve, guaranteeing the First Amendment a continuing role in the public agenda.

Perhaps no policy area reveals the nature of American constitutional democracy as well as the issue of church-state relations. In this chapter, which describes the conduct of contemporary policymaking in the area of religion and politics, several features of the U.S. system stand out in clear relief. Among these are the central but limited role of public opinion, and the importance of state and local governments as sources of policy innovation and change. Questions of religious establishment and free exercise evoke, in the most fundamental way, the importance of a nonelected federal judiciary. Lastly, the separation of powers among the elected branches of the federal government results in a great deal of congressional activity that is generally ineffective and in an unusual degree of passivity in the executive branch. The differential types of representation created by a locally recruited and elected U.S. House of Representatives, as well as by the biases inherent in the Electoral College, provide a fascinating study in contrasts among various political actors' approaches to the political role of religion.

Public Opinion

Throughout the history of democratic theory, there has been a vigorous debate about the quality of the political understanding of ordinary citizens. The question, simply put, is whether or not "the people" are actually capable of self-government.

Not surprisingly, this question has occasioned a great deal of research. The frequency of such research increased in the post–World War II era, when the use of public opinion surveys became commonplace. Although scholarly analyses have not definitively answered the question of citizen competence, most observers agree that the public typically does not have an interest in or knowledge of the details of most issues of public policy (Asher 1992; Zaller 1992). It is also commonly accepted that the popular understanding of policy issues generally is not as complex or as nuanced as that among political elites; but the gap between the two groups varies from issue to issue. On certain issues, such as abortion or race relations, many citizens have relatively stable, intense preferences, whereas in regard to most others, public knowledge or concern may be weak or nonexistent.

In view of public survey findings, it is rather unlikely that arcane legal considerations about religious establishment or free exercise often penetrate the consciousness of ordinary citizens. Nevertheless, the American public does appear to have reasonably coherent, well-formed attitudes about church-state relations.[1] As will become clear from the discussion in this chapter, such attitudes are not necessarily "consistent" in any logical or ideological sense. American attitudes about church-state relations are subject to two conflicting forces. First, as we observed in Chapter 1, Americans are highly religious. Compared with citizens of other industrialized nations, Americans report an unusually high degree of religious belief, affiliation, and practice. This means that, periodically, there is a strong temptation on the part of some citizens to translate their religious principles into public policy. That is, if religion is an important influence in a citizen's life, that citizen seems more likely to seek government endorsement of religiously based values. Second, and perhaps conversely, the concept of a constitutional "separation of church and state" (a phrase that appears nowhere in the U.S. Constitution) is a powerful positive symbol in American political discourse. Although there is little agreement concerning the precise meaning of such separation, the principle itself is not generally contested in American politics.

The content of public attitudes on church-state relations can be summarized rather easily. At the abstract, symbolic level, there is ample support for separatist views of the Establishment Clause and libertarian views of the Free Exercise Clause, although such support is by no means unanimous. Recent research has suggested that nearly two-thirds of Americans endorse a "high wall of separation" between church and state, although only about half reject any government help to religion at all (Jelen and Wilcox 1995, 59). On Free Exercise questions, a survey of residents in the District of Columbia showed a near unanimity of agreement that "people have the right to practice their religion as they see fit, even if their practices seem strange to most Americans." However, support for religious free exercise dropped dramatically when the question of lawbreaking was raised: Only 21 percent disagreed with the statement "It is important for people to obey the law, even if it means limiting their religious freedom" (Jelen and Wilcox 1995, 115). Thus, when questions of church-state relations are posed at the level of general principles, strong support for libertarian and separatist views of the Free Exercise and Establishment clauses, respectively, is observed. However, the sensitivity of these attitudes to variations in the wording of survey questions is also noteworthy, suggesting that public attitudes on these issues may not be well formed (Labow 1980). However, church-state separation and individual liberty are clearly powerful positive symbols for many, if not most, Americans.

With respect to concrete applications of the First Amendment clauses on religion, public attitudes are more complex. Regarding questions of religious establishment, many Americans appear to distinguish among public displays of religious symbols (such as Christmas decorations on public property), financial support for religious institutions, and religious socialization in public schools. In the above-mentioned survey, Free Exercise attitudes were similarly structured, with respondents making distinctions among the Free Exercise rights of groups they considered dangerous (e.g., "cultists," Satanists, and the like); groups they considered strange but harmless (e.g., students who sought to wear religious apparel in public schools); and immigrant groups. Attitudes concerning concrete issues of religious establishment were organized around an activity-based heuristic, whereas attitudes toward free exercise of religion seemed structured around a group-based belief system: In other words, with respect to questions of religious establishment, respondents cared most about *what* it was that religiously motivated people were doing. In the realm of free exercise, what seemed to matter most was *who* was exercising religious freedom. This apparent inconsistency is not imputable to a lack of sophistication among mass publics (Converse 1964), because the attitude structures of a variety of elite populations (leaders in politics, business, religion, and communications) are similar to those of ordinary citizens. Attitudes expressed toward church-state relations are not necessarily consistent in either group.

Many Americans appear to be abstract separatists but concrete accommodationists. Some survey respondents endorsed the general principle of church-state separation but expressed support for prayer in public schools, tuition tax vouchers, and publicly funded Nativity scenes. Similarly, with respect to issues involving religious free exercise, many Americans are abstract libertarians but concrete communalists. That is, they have a tendency to endorse the principle of the free exercise of religion in the abstract but express willingness to restrict a variety of religiously motivated practices, such as the ritual use of hallucinogenic drugs by

Native Americans, religious solicitation at airports, and allowing adherents of minority religions (such as Jews) time off work on religious holidays.

A disparity between public support for a general principle and public willingness to apply the principle in concrete instances has been noted by scholars in various contexts (see Prothro and Grigg 1960; Zaller 1992). With respect to church-state issues, the inconsistency appears to result from a lack of familiarity with the range of possible applications of the First Amendment. Genuine religious diversity is not part of the experience of most Americans.

In 1994, I formed several focus groups with the purpose of exploring these patterns in greater depth. Focus groups are often used in research into public opinion. They generally involve long, relatively unstructured conversations with a number of selected individuals. In the informal context of a focus group—without the (possibly) artificial structure of a survey questionnaire—respondents can express themselves more freely. The focus group technique also allows respondents to speak to one another and to change their minds in response to conversations with other participants or with the researcher.

I found it remarkably easy to persuade my focus group respondents to switch from religious accommodationism to a more separatist stance by confronting them with the possibility of genuine religious diversity. A number of proponents of school prayer changed their views when confronted with the possibility that a contemporary classroom might contain polytheists (e.g., Hindus). These respondents conceded the difficulty of composing a nondenominational prayer with such students included in the group. When respondents were presented with various scenarios for compromise among different religious groups in this context, the notion of "positive neutrality" seemed much less attractive to them. Most respondents, for example, were not willing to rotate prayers to accommodate members of different religious traditions. As one respondent put it, "I don't want my children praying to Buddha" (Jelen and Wilcox 1995, 152). When a specific issue involving government support for religion is raised, many individuals were not aware that a constitutional principle was at stake; nor did they seem cognizant of the extent of religious diversity within the United States.

In sum, public opinion on questions of church-state relations is generally coherent but not consistent. Symbols of religious freedom and church-state separation receive high levels of support among mass publics, but many Americans are accommodationist on questions of establishment, and communalist on questions involving religious free exercise. This apparent inconsistency across levels of analysis has important implications for the practice of religious politics in the United States. The fact that Americans generally hold both meaningfully accommodationist and separatist values suggests that activists on both sides of the debate have resources with which to compete, and that such elites can plausibly claim popular support for their positions on church-state issues.

Interest Groups

At any given moment, and with respect to any particular issue, a bewildering variety of organized interest groups are attempting to influence public policy with respect to some aspect of church-state relations (for overviews, see Hofrenning 1995; Hertzke 1988, 1989; and Fowler, Hertzke, and Olson 1998). Groups on the theological right include Christian Coalition, Focus on the Family, **Catholic Alliance, Concerned Women for America,** and the Eagle Forum; and on the left, **Pax Christi, Bread for the World,** and **Evangelicals for Social Action.** Other groups do not fit neatly into the conventional categories of "liberal" and "conservative." For example, the organization **JustLife** generally takes a liberal position on the death penalty, gun control, and military spending, but a conservative stance on abortion and euthanasia. Further, many organizations take what might be called pragmatic positions on church-state issues. For example, the United States Catholic Conference traditionally has taken a separatist position on the issue of school prayer, and an accommodationist position with respect to tax vouchers for private school tuition. In both instances, the USCC is responding to the interests of its religious constituency.

However, only a few groups were organized with the primary purpose of exerting an influence on the relationship between church and state. Several of these— the **American Civil Liberties Union (ACLU), People for the American Way (PAW),** and Americans United for the Separation of Church and State (AUSCS)—have focused their attention on perceived violations of the Establishment Clause and generally have taken separatist positions. These groups have tended to confine their attention to legal work and public education (Murley 1988)—monitoring and publicizing legislation and court decisions, and filing *amicus curiae* briefs in specific court cases.

With respect to strategy and tactics, there are some notable differences between the groups listed above. The AUSCS and PAW have concerned themselves almost exclusively with questions of religious establishment. In contrast, the American Civil Liberties Union is a much older organization with a considerably broader agenda. The ACLU has been active in protecting the Free Exercise right of religious minorities, and has historically been the object of scathing criticism from conservative Christian organizations (Wills 1990). In terms of the classification scheme developed in the first chapter, the ACLU might be characterized as a free-marketeer organization, whereas PAW and AUSCS have assumed a stance of religious minimalism.

These groups tend to operate at something of a disadvantage because of the disparity between abstract support for separatism and concrete public support for specific governmental policies that appear to accommodate religious belief. Even direct mail appeals, which are presumably sent to group members or sympathizers, often contain detailed explanations of why apparently innocuous policies are subversive of church-state separation. For example, a recent issue of *Church and State* (a publication of the AUSCS) contained a long article detailing why a proposed "Religious Freedom Amendment" to the Constitution would actually be subversive of religious freedom (Boston 1997). Given the high level of legitimacy enjoyed by religious belief in the United States, separatist groups seem to have the more difficult case to make. It is perhaps not surprising that such groups have been limited to public education and litigation, given the relative unpopularity of separatism applied to concrete instances. Because it is so difficult to make a case for specific separatist policies at the grass roots, it is not surprising that the ACLU and AUSCS have tended to focus their efforts toward the elite level.

For example, a recent mailing from AUSCS (December 1997) attempted to educate group members as to the dangers of the Religious Freedom Amendment, which was motivated by the Supreme Court rulings in *Smith* and *Bourne:*

> The legislative wrecking ball you know as the ill-named "Religious Freedom Amendment" (RFA) is poised to crush the wall of separation between church and state. . . . *Last month, . . . the House Constitution Subcommittee pushed the RFA through the House Judiciary Committee.* This is the first time in the long, dangerous history of the amendment that extremist lawmakers have been able to push it to a vote. And the minute Congress returns, the proponents of this dangerous amendment will put it on a fast track. . . . RFA supporters have mounted a massive campaign to bamboozle their fellow lawmakers, the media, and the American public that passage of the amendment would be of no consequence. *But you know that the consequences are many and severe.* . . . RFA would destroy America's tradition of freedom of conscience and demolish the wall of separation between church and state. [Emphasis in original.]

This mailing takes on the formidable task of showing that (according to the AUSCS) a constitutional amendment designed to protect religious freedom would do the exact opposite. A group that opposes school prayer, tuition tax vouchers, and other accommodationist proposals has essentially been put on the defensive by the accommodationists' appropriation of the symbol "religious freedom." To accomplish this, the AUSCS invokes language involving the symbol of

TABLE 3.1   Church-State Organizations on the Web

Christian Coalition	www.cc.org
Rutherford Institute	www.rutherford.org
American Center for Law and Justice	www.aclj.org
American Civil Liberties Union	www.aclu.com
Americans United for the Separation of Church and State	www.au.org
People for the American Way	www.pfaw.org

church-state separation, and suggests that the RFA is in fact designed to subvert the Establishment Clause.

Conversely, accommodationist groups such as Moral Majority and (more recently) Christian Coalition have been able to compete in a wider political arena. Some accommodationist groups, such as the **American Center for Law and Justice** and the **Rutherford Institute,** have focused on litigation to counteract the activities of separatist groups. Other organizations, such as Christian Coalition, have proved effective at lobbying the legislatures at various levels of government as well as at campaigning for the election of candidates they support (Wilcox 1996; Moen 1989). To the extent that such groups have been able to focus public attention on the *application* of the religion clauses of the First Amendment, it is not surprising that these more accommodationist groups have directed their efforts at the mobilization of public opinion and the persuasion of elected officials.

In particular, accommodationists have had an easier time making the public connection between their positions on constitutional issues and widely held values such as liberty and democracy. For example, it is instructive to contrast the Christian Coalition's account of the Religious Freedom Amendment with that of Americans United for the Separation of Church and State.

> Thursday, June 4, marked the first time in 27 years that the House of Representatives held a vote on an amendment to the Constitution to permit school prayer. The Religious Freedom Amendment (H.J. Res. 78) fell short of the necessary two-thirds majority to pass a Constitutional Amendment. . . . The majority of the House, in a bipartisan fashion, voted for the Religious Freedom Amendment. This reflects the importance that America places on religious liberties and how the courts have been rolling back those rights for the last 36 years. (Christian Coalition 1998)

Christian Coalition used the language of free exercise and invoked positive symbols such as "majority," "bipartisanship," and religious liberties. Christian Coalition did not find it necessary to characterize their opponents as "extremists," or "dangerous," nor did it seem necessary to characterize the lobbying efforts of anyone as "bamboozling." Again, given the popularity of accommodationist positions at the applied level, those who would favor a narrow reading of the Establishment Clause do appear to enjoy a rhetorical advantage.

The actual effectiveness of religious interest groups is the subject of some dispute. Matthew Moen has asserted that although the Christian Right has fallen short of its goal of transforming the nature of American politics, various Christian Right organizations have become entrenched in state and local party organizations and have achieved some notable legislative successes (Moen 1992). Christian Coalition appears to have been particularly effective in influencing the actions of local legislatures and school boards, and has generally shifted its focus from national politics to the state and local levels.

Religious interest groups that have been granted tax-exempt status—as instituted by Congress under the Free Exercise Clause—are limited in the tactics they may employ to influence policy: Overt electioneering, direct lobbying of Congress, or partisan activity (e.g., campaign contributions to candidates or parties, explicit electoral endorsements, and the like) may result in the revocation of their tax exemptions. Thus, although some groups (e.g., Christian Coalition) appear to press the boundaries of such limitations, the political activities of many religiously motivated interest groups are legally restricted.

The effectiveness of religious interest groups may be limited by two additional factors, relating to the representational claims made by such groups. First, many highly religious people regard separation as the appropriate relationship between church and state. Roger Williams, a prominent member of the clergy during Colonial times, argued that anything less than a strong wall of separation between church and state was likely to have a contaminating effect on religious belief and practice (Wills 1990; Segers and Jelen 1998). Such attitudes have persisted to the present day. Analyses of contemporary public opinion (Jelen and Wilcox 1997) suggest that respondents who exhibit the tendencies of religious minimalism, described in Chapter 1 (separatist on establishment questions, and communalist on issues involving free exercise), are not generally secular or irreligious. Nonreligious or non-Christian respondents are found predominantly in the religious free-marketeer category. In contrast, a large number of religious minimalists are devout, orthodox Baptists who hold their political views on church-state separation for theological reasons rather than constitutional ones (Jelen and Wilcox 1997). Thus, activists who promote an accommodationist view of questions of religious establishment may lack popular support among their ostensible constituents.

A second consideration relates to the effects of religious particularism. In a very perceptive analysis, Roger Finke and Rodney Stark (1992) have suggested that the extent of religious observance (church membership, attendance, etc.) is to a large extent a function of religious competition. That is, in areas and periods dominated by a single religious tradition, there is a tendency for religious organizations to become "lazy" and to fail to respond to the needs and desires of potential members. Conversely, in religiously pluralistic environments, in which potential church members can choose among a variety of denominations, churches must compete for members. Such competition is thought to require clergy to accommodate the preferences of laypersons, and accommodation appears to have a positive effect on religious observance.

From the Finke-Stark account it may follow that churches in religiously competitive environments have incentives to engage in what might be termed product differentiation. That is, churches that are competing for members may attempt to distinguish themselves from their religious rivals, and indeed, may devote most of their attention to distancing themselves from similar religious traditions. In an earlier publication based on empirical research, I reported that the pastors of certain Baptist congregations in a Midwestern community were extremely precise in distinguishing themselves from other Baptist traditions. For example, one pastor, who was affiliated with the General Association of Regular Baptist Churches (GARBC), provided me with a long, detailed history of his denomination, and carefully explained how the GARBC was different from and superior to the American Baptist Church and the Southern Baptist Convention (Jelen 1993).

If this sort of behavior is typical, as the Finke-Stark account suggests, it may follow that the logic of religious recruitment runs counter to that of political mobilization. That is, political cooperation between members of diverse religious traditions may require that theological differences be submerged and minimized. However, the imperatives of congregational life may entail the requirement that religious differences be emphasized and contrasted as clearly as possible. It would be difficult for religious leaders to disparage the beliefs of members of different denominations in religious settings and simultaneously to encourage political cooperation with such religious outsiders. Given the probable necessity of ecumenical coalitions and the difficulty of maintaining such partnerships among highly religious people, many religiously devout citizens may have decided to forgo religiously motivated political activity.

Thus, different organizations may take distinctive positions on issues relating to religious establishment and free exercise. In terms of the typology developed in Chapter 1, we might classify interests groups as shown in Figure 3.1:

FIGURE 3.1　Classification of Selected Interest Groups on Church-State Issues

		Establishment Clause	
		Accommodationist	*Separationist*
	Communalist	*Christian Preferentialist* Moral Majority	*Religious Minimalist* Americans United for the Separation of Church and State
Free *Exercise* *Clause*	*Libertarian*	*Religious Nonpreferentialist* American Center for 　Law and Justice Christian Coalition Rutherford Institute	*Religious Free-Marketer* American Civil 　Liberties Union People for the 　American Way

As noted earlier, the ACLU might fall into the free-marketeer category, due to its libertarian stance on the Free Exercise Clause. Further, as we will see in Chapter 4 in more detail, Christian Right organizations such as Moral Majority, which could legitimately be classified as Christian preferentialists, have given way to newer groups like Christian Coalition, which appear to occupy a more nonpreferentialist position. The difference, of course, is attributable to the organizations' distinctive views on the meaning of the Free Exercise Clause. In Chapter 4, I suggest ways in which the changing interpretation of religious free exercise has shaped the agenda of religious conservatives in the 1990s.

State and Local Government

The late Thomas P. "Tip" O'Neill is said to have observed that "all politics is local." Any observer of contemporary church-state relations would discern a good deal of truth in that assertion. In a large majority of cases, controversy over the proper relationship between politics and religion is raised by the actions of government at the state or local level. The political arenas in which church-state relations are most often contested are state legislatures, county boards, city or village councils, or local school boards. The grassroots character of most church-state contests is not be surprising. After all, most citizens have more direct contact with their local government bodies than with the relatively remote federal agencies in Washington. "Retail" or small-scale religious politics often involves questions of aesthetics, zoning, local taxation, or public education. A very high percentage of church-state questions deal with the education of schoolchildren, which has typically been the province of local governments.

Such localized concerns have attained the status of constitutional issues, in large part, because of the doctrine of "incorporation" (Levy 1986, 1988; Friendly and Elliot 1984). As we saw in the preceding chapter, the Bill of Rights (including the religion clauses of the First Amendment) is a set of prohibitions on the powers of *Congress,* or more generally, on the federal government. However, the strict distinction between restrictions on the federal government and those applicable to subnational governments has eroded steadily since the Civil War. Over a period of time, the Bill of Rights has been "incorporated" to include state and local governments. The scope of the doctrine of incorporation remains controversial (Anastopolo 1981); but there is now general agreement that the religion clauses of the First Amendment properly apply to the actions of subnational governments as well as to the federal government.

The raising of constitutional issues by state and local governments occurs rather frequently in part because of the particular contours of public opinion. Recall that many Americans are abstract separationists but concrete accommodationists. When local governments deal with issues such as Sabbath observances, holiday displays with religious themes, or school curricula, they are responding to signals from local communities in which many individuals may be unaware of the general constitutional principle at stake. Mass publics tend to seek the presumed benefits of religious accommodation without seriously considering the possible conflicts between their actions and the U.S. Constitution. For example, residents of a local school district in which parents are concerned about juvenile delinquency may desire organized public prayer or the posting of the Ten Commandments in schools, as reminders of a shared moral and ethical framework. The pressing goal of reducing antisocial behavior on the part of adolescents may seem much more important than a particular reading of a constitutional provision.

On church-state issues, accommodationist public opinion is likely to be quite formidable at the subnational level. Not only are accommodationist positions generally rather popular (Murley 1988; Elifson and Hadaway 1985), but recent research has shown that churches are important sources of political learning (Jelen 1991; Wald et al. 1988). The socializing effects of religious observance are strongest in evangelical, pietistic congregations, which are also the most favorably disposed toward the teaching of creationism, school prayer, and the like (Elifson and Hadaway 1985; Wald et al. 1990). Citizens who hold separatist viewpoints are not typically members of such congregations; and because they lack opportunities for comparable social interaction, they may come to regard themselves as politically isolated on such issues (Noelle-Neuman 1993). Thus, even if separatist opinions are relatively widespread, they are less likely to be expressed than are accommodationist perspectives.

Because subnational governments tend to feel a greater need to respond to local public opinion, local officials often pass and enforce measures that seemingly violate the Establishment or Free Exercise clauses. The local electoral incentives to pass popular measures that involve Establishment issues tend to be strong; in contrast, any popular sanctions against officials for having passed legislation later overturned as unconstitutional tend to be weak (Parsons 1997). Even more typically, issues involving the Free Exercise Clause often involve the religious rights of small, unpopular, and politically impotent minorities. It would take either a great deal of political courage or a political death wish for a state or local official to vote in favor of the rights of Native Americans to ingest peyote, or of Muslim immigrants to engage in female "circumcision" (a genital alteration that typically has dire health consequences for women) (Dugger 1996).

In sum, then, state and local governments have many opportunities to make policies that indirectly invoke the constitutional provisions on religion. To the extent that subnational governments are responsive to "visible" public opinion, they have strong incentives to pass measures that are generally accommodationist on issues involving religious establishment, and communalist with respect to questions of religious free exercise. In terms of the typology developed above, state and local policymaking in most areas of the United States is likely to take on a Christian preferentialist cast.

The Supreme Court

Because the church-state relationship involves questions of constitutional importance, the courts (especially the Supreme Court) are the most frequent arenas in which such issues are contested. The courts typically become involved when the legality of policies made at the state and local levels are disputed. They often have overruled popular local majorities in favor of the rights of religiously defined minorities.

With respect to the Establishment Clause, the Supreme Court has typically taken a separatist position, beginning most recently with the Court's opinions in *Everson v. Board of Education* and *Engel v. Vitale*. In particular, *Engel* (the Court's first decision banning organized school prayer) has generated a great deal of controversy and congressional reaction.

At present, the operative (and controversial) precedent is *Lemon v. Kurtzman*, in which Warren Burger proposed a three-pronged test to determine whether the Establishment Clause has been violated by an act of government. The *Lemon* test would require that a policy be invalidated if it has the purpose or the effect of either advancing or inhibiting religion, or entails an "excessive entanglement" between government and religion (Jelen and Wilcox 1995, 18; Wald 1997). A government policy must be declared unconstitutional if it fulfills *any* of these conditions. Furthermore, the *Lemon* test applies all government entanglements with religion generally—not only to governmental advancement or inhibition of a particular denomination.

Thus, the Supreme Court has generally held that governmental policies that assist religious institutions or advance religious beliefs are unconstitutional. The Court has struck down measures that would require public schools to devote "equal time" to the teaching of creationism and evolution *(Edwards v. Aguillard)*, as well as several efforts to promote prayer in public schools (Murley 1988). Most recently, the court disallowed an Alabama measure mandating a "moment of silence" in public schools *(Wallace v. Jaffree)*, as well as "voluntary" prayer at a high school graduation ceremony *(Lee v. Weisman)*. The Court has also held that governmental assistance to religious schools must be narrowly defined and have a clear secular purpose. For example, it is generally considered constitutional for a state government to provide mathematics textbooks, because the state has a legitimate secular purpose in promoting mathematics instruction. However, general state assistance to parochial schools, or providing instructors, would be unconstitutional *(Abingdon Township School District v. Schempp; County of Allegheny v. ACLU; Aguilar v. Felton)*. The Court has since permitted some limited provision of public school instructors to parochial schools (in the process modifying, but not overruling, *Aguilar*) in the 1997 case of *Agostini v. Felton*.

Outside the area of public education, the Court has consistently ruled that holiday Nativity scenes with specifically religious themes are unconstitutional if created or funded by local government authorities (Jelen and Wilcox 1995). Most recently, in *Schundler v. American Civil Liberties Union* (1997), the Court allowed to stand a lower court ruling that banned (on Establishment grounds) a holiday display containing a Nativity scene, a Hanukkah menorah, and a Christmas tree (Greenhouse 1997). The Court made a distinction between a specifically "religious" display and one involving a general "holiday" season observance. At this writing, it is not clear whether a depiction of a Christmas tree or Santa Claus is necessary to offset the religious messages of the menorah or Nativity scene; but the language used in *Schundler* does not appear to be moving in a more accommodationist direction.

The apparent vagueness of *Schundler* aside, the Court has more recently appeared to relax its strict separatist interpretation of *Lemon*. The Court has permitted state funding for a sign-language interpreter for a deaf student enrolled in a parochial school *(Zobrest v. Catalina Foothills School District)*, and has required public schools to permit religious groups to use school facilities after hours if such opportunities are extended to nonreligious groups *(Lamb's Chapel v. Center Moriches Union Free School District)*. However, there appears to have been no general movement in the Court toward a more accommodationist reading of the Constitution, nor any serious attempt to overrule or seriously modify *Lemon*.[2]

Until recently, the Supreme Court has traditionally taken a libertarian stance toward issues involving the Free Exercise Clause (Brisbin 1992; Way and Burt 1983). Although the right to the free exercise of religion has never been absolute, the Court has generally been willing to protect the prerogatives of unconventional religious groups. Thomas Robbins has suggested that the Court has historically adopted a three-part test for evaluating the constitutionality of claims involving the Free Exercise Clause. The criteria in question were derived from *Sherbert v. Verner* (1963) and *Wisconsin v. Yoder* (1972). In *Sherbert*, the Court held that a state's denial of unemployment benefits to a plaintiff who refused to work on the Sabbath constituted a violation of that person's religious liberty under the Free Exercise Clause, despite the fact that most recipients of government unemployment benefits will be stripped of such support for refusing an offer of employment. The Court's ruling in *Yoder* supported the claim of an Amish family (a religious sect that rejects much of the technology and social organization of the industrial world) to reject Wisconsin's compulsory education law (and to remove their children from school at the age of 14, rather than the statutory minimum of 16), as a legitimate exercise of the family's right of religious free exercise.

Under the three-pronged *Sherbert-Yoder* test, government must show that "it has a compelling interest which justifies the abridgment of the right to free exercise of religion" (Pfeffer 1967). Government regulations that inhibit religious freedom traditionally have been subjected to strict scrutiny by the courts, and must be demonstrably *essential* in order to justify the abridgment of religious freedom. Needless to say, this is a formidable hurdle, as government bears the substantial burden of proof.

If the centrality of purpose of a particular government regulation of religious practice has been established, the burden of proof under *Sherbert-Yoder* shifts to the plaintiff—the persons or groups claiming that their religious freedom has been violated. Given the established importance of a government regulation, a religious practice must be "central" to the religion under consideration, and the government regulation must involve a "substantial infringement" on that practice. This is the second prong of the *Sherbert-Yoder* test.

Lastly, courts generally consider whether a compelling government regulation that restricts religious free exercise is the "least restrictive alternative" available by which the state might achieve its secular goals. A policy might well be deemed unconstitutional if government objectives can be achieved by less intrusive means.

The stringency with which the "compelling state interest" test has been applied perhaps can be seen most clearly in the case of military conscription. It must be emphasized that religious exemptions from compulsory military service were created by Congress, and the Supreme Court has never asserted a constitutional *right* to conscientious objection. Nevertheless, the Court has permitted conscientious objection to military service on religious grounds—which it has defined broadly to include personal codes of morality (*United States v. Seeger* [1965]; *Welsh v. United States* [1970])—although the defense of the nation is considered an "essential" government function.[3] The Court did not discover or create a "right" to the status of conscientious objector, but it has drastically extended the scope of Congress's provision.

Under the Rehnquist Court, judicial deference to free exercise claims appears to be waning. In *Employment Division v. Smith* (1990) the Court ruled that Native Americans who used the hallucinogenic drug peyote during a religious ritual were not entitled to legal protection under the Free Exercise Clause. In the Court's majority opinion, Antonin Scalia wrote that actions that would otherwise be prohibited by a state's criminal code are not accorded special protection for religious reasons unless such an exception has been made explicit by the state's legislature (Savage 1993). Under the Court's ruling in *Smith,* the criterion for protection of an otherwise restricted practice under the Free Exercise Clause appears to have moved away from the compelling state interest standard of *Sherbert-Yoder* toward a more communalist understanding of the Free Exercise Clause (Brisbin 1992). The *Smith* decision, which is consistent with an accommodationist reading of the Establishment Clause, may signal that the Court is according legislative acts (and by extension, popular majorities) increasing deference. The implications of *Smith* have occupied the attention of the U.S. Congress in recent years.

The majority opinion in *Smith* emphasized the continuity between the *Smith* decision and earlier free exercise jurisprudence, as well as limiting the scope of earlier decisions. Scalia argued in *Smith* that since the Free Exercise Clause applies to religious conduct as well as religious expression, it is inappropriate (and indeed, unrealistic) to apply the standard of "compelling state interest" to free exercise questions. Under the compelling state interest standard, governments can regulate protected activities only if such regulation is absolutely essential to the functioning of government. Clearly, this is a very high standard, which most government regulations fail to meet.

Scalia went on to argue that other freedoms were involved besides the free exercise of religion. For example, in the 1943 case of *West Virginia State Board of Education v. Barnette,* which involved the question of mandatory flag salutes for Jehovah's Witnesses in public schools, Scalia suggested that the regulation in question involved issues of free speech as well as of free exercise of religion. Scalia's majority opinion in *Smith* suggests that when applied to questions of religiously motivated conduct, the government's burden in free exercise cases is much less rigorous than had previously been believed.[4]

In 1997, the Court reaffirmed its ruling in *Smith* (and overturned the Religious Freedom Restoration Act passed by Congress) in *City of Boerne v. Flores.* In *Boerne* (pronounced "Bernie"), a Roman Catholic church located in a historic district in the city of Boerne, Texas (a small city near San Antonio), sought permission to expand its chapel in response to the growth of the congregation. The city denied its application for expansion, citing the power of municipal government to maintain the architectural character of the older area of the city. Citing the Religious Freedom Restoration Act (described in the following section), the archdiocese of San Antonio sued the city, arguing that Boerne did not have a "compelling interest" in historic preservation. The Supreme Court, by a margin of 6-3, ruled the RFRA unconstitutional, because Congress had exceeded its authority by changing the substantive meaning of the Free Exercise Clause (from that defined by the Court in *Smith*). Although the enforcement section of the Fourteenth Amendment ("Congress shall have the power to enforce this Amendment with appropriate legislation") allows Congress to correct obvious constitutional violations, it does not permit Congress to define the nature of the Bill of Rights.

Thus, the Court has taken a more or less consistently separatist position with respect to the Establishment Clause, and despite Scalia's efforts to demonstrate continuity, appears to have shifted from a libertarian to a communalist position on issues involving the free exercise of religion. In terms of the typology developed in Figure 3.1, the Court has moved from a religious free-marketeer stance toward one of religious minimalism.

Congress

Congress has not typically been proactive in enacting legislation with respect to church-state relations. For the most part, the role of Congress has been to react (usually ineffectually) to decisions of the Supreme Court. Because Congress is a popularly elected branch of the federal government, members of Congress have frequently sought to respond to accommodationist public opinion. However, due perhaps to the religious diversity represented in Congress, as well as to the extraordinary majorities required to pass Constitutional Amendments, most congressional efforts to counteract separatist decisions of the Supreme Court have not been successful.

Much of Congress's attention in the area of church-state relations has been devoted to the perennial issue of school prayer. Because school prayer is likely an "easy" issue[5] (Carmines and Stimson 1980) and because most Americans favor some form of school prayer, members of Congress have frequently sought to pass amendments to bills, House and Senate resolutions, and the Constitution that would permit the practice. Since the *Engel* decision in 1962, near 100 such measures have been introduced in the Senate and several hundred have been introduced in the House (Murley 1988). Most of the constitutional amendments in question have used the language of free exercise, emphasizing the voluntary or noncoercive aspects of school prayer. A proposed amendment, introduced by Senators Strom Thurmond (R.-S.C.), Orrin G. Hatch (R.-Utah), Lawton Chiles (D.-Fla.), James Abdnor (R.-S.D.), Don Nickles (R.-Okla.), and Jesse A. Helms (R.-N.C.), is typical of the genre: "Nothing in this Constitution shall be construed to prohibit individual or group prayer in public schools or other public institutions. No person shall be required by the United States or any state to participate in prayer. Neither the United States nor any state shall compose the words of any prayer to be said in public schools."[6] Typically, such measures are supported by majorities in each house of Congress but fall short of the two-thirds vote required to pass an amendment to the Constitution. In other cases, members of Congress have attempted to remove issues of school prayer from the Supreme Court's appellate jurisdiction, but these have thus far been unsuccessful.

The pattern of Congress's responding to rulings of the federal courts has continued in other areas as well. Early in 1997, House Republicans introduced a "sense of Congress" resolution, backing a judge who had refused (contrary to earlier precedent and a court order) to remove a display of the Ten Commandments from his courtroom (Seelye 1997). This resolution is nonbinding and lacks the force of law, but it can be seen as an attempt to acknowledge the accommodationist strand in public opinion.

In 1993, Congress passed the Religious Freedom Restoration Act (RFRA), which was a legislative attempt to reverse the Court's ruling in *Smith* and to reinstate the compelling state interest standard in cases involving religious free exercise. The RFRA explicitly restored the compelling state interest test as applied in *Sherbert* and *Yoder,* and would forbid government at all levels from "substantially burden(ing) a person's free exercise of religion unless government can show that the burden is (1) in furtherance of a compelling government interest and (2) is the least restrictive means of furthering that . . . interest" (Greenhouse 1997). As noted earlier, this measure was overturned by the Supreme Court in the *Boerne* case, in 1997.

In response to the Court's ruling in *Boerne,* Congress is as of this writing considering another measure, titled the Religious Liberty Protection Act (RLPA). Like the RFRA, the RLPA is aimed at restoring the *Sherbert-Yoder* test to Free Exercise cases. In the case of the RLPA, Congress derives its constitutional authority to pass such a measure from the Commerce Clause, and from Congress's spending power under Article 1 of the Constitution. Under the Commerce Clause, Congress has a great deal of discretion in the regulation of commercial transactions between states, and some analysts believe that this will provide a stronger basis for congressional reversal of *Smith* and *Boerne* than Congress's enforcement power under the Fourteenth Amendment.[7]

Lastly, Rep. Ernest J. Istook, Jr. (R.-Okla.) has proposed a constitutional amendment that would, to a large extent, enact an accommodationist interpretation of the Establishment Clause. The proposed amendment reads:

> To secure the people's right to acknowledge God according to the dictates of conscience; the people's right to pray and to recognize their religious beliefs, heritage, or traditions on public property, including schools, shall not be infringed. The government shall not require any person to join in prayer or other religious activity, initiate or designate school prayers, discriminate against religion, or deny a benefit to religion. (Boston 1997)

As is typical of recent congressional measures, the predominant tone of Istook's amendment is one of concern for religious free exercise. However, in its prohibition against state discrimination with regard to religion, or state denial of benefits to religion, it is considerably broader in scope than the school prayer amendments that have been offered in the past. Presumably, an amendment to the Constitution would eliminate the problem of judicial review, since the Constitution itself cannot (by definition) be held unconstitutional. Unfortunately for proponents of the measure, the House of Representatives defeated the Istook amendment in 1998. In a vote taken on June 4 of that year, 224 voted in favor, and 203 voted against the measure. The affirmative vote fell well short of the two-thirds majority required to pass constitutional amendments.[8] Istook, presumably in deference to his Oklahoma constituency, reintroduced the measure, with the same wording, on September 15, 1999 (Americans United for the Separation of Church and State 1999). In late 1999, the matter was still pending in the House of Representatives.

Given the frequency with which local governments attempt to accommodate religious belief in public institutions, as well as the general popularity of an accommodationist reading of the Establishment Clause (and the highly positive symbol of religious free exercise), it is not clear why congressional attempts to amend the Constitution have not been successful. Most likely, congressional impotence on this set of issues results from the reluctance of some members to revise the Constitution (which, in a **civil religion** sense, might be regarded as a "sacred" document), as well as from the religious diversity represented in the national legislature. Members of mainline Protestant denominations, as well as Catholics, Jews, and non-Christians, have generally been indifferent or hostile to the Christian preferentialist tendencies of some local governments (Murley 1988); and the representation of such religious groups in Congress may have been sufficient to prevent the formation of the extraordinary majority needed to amend the Constitution.

One might well ask why this issue is continually resurrected in Congress, given the apparent futility of such attempts. The answer appears to lie in the decentralized nature of Congress, and the importance of local factors in congressional elections. Political parties in Congress are characterized by low levels of **party discipline;** that is, the party leaders in Congress (or the White House) have limited means of gaining support for their proposals from the congressional rank and file. Rather, since congressional candidates are self-recruited and run in state or local constituencies, successful candidates are typically quite attentive to the desires and preferences of their constituents. What this means is that individual members of Congress may find it politically beneficial to introduce or support highly visible legislation (such as constitutional amendments), even if such measures have little chance of being enacted. Thus, members of Congress who represent districts or states in which visible public support for religion is politically popular, or in which issues such as school prayer have been raised, may enhance their prospects for re-election with such a strategy. This type of maneuver is more typically practiced by members of the House of Representatives, who often represent smaller and more homogeneous constituencies than do members of the Senate.

In sum, one can say with certainty that within certain subnational jurisdictions, entrepreneurial political leaders believe they can make political gains by appearing to represent accommodationist public opinion in Congress. Thus, measures that apparently support the rights of religious free exercise and narrow the scope of the Establishment Clause seem likely to be permanent features of the congressional landscape. However, the diversity of Congress, as well as the large majorities needed to pass constitutional amendments, have rendered such efforts ineffective.

The Executive Branch

Typically, issues involving religious establishment and free exercise have not been high priorities for U.S. presidents (Murley 1988). With the exception of Ronald Reagan (to be discussed below), few presidents since *Engel* have made strong pronouncements, or attempted policy initiatives, on the religion clauses of the First Amendment.

Since 1964 (the first presidential election after *Engel*), Republican party platforms have routinely offered support for school prayer, whereas Democratic platforms have generally ignored the issue (Murley 1988). This contrast doubtlessly reflects religious differences in the activist stratum of the two parties, which began to emerge as a result of the candidacy of conservative Republican Barry Goldwater (Guth and Green 1989). However, once elected, U.S. presidents of both parties have done little more than offer symbolic support for religion, and have not offered public appeals for specific policies. For example, President Bush invoked religious values in his "thousand points of light" speech; and President Clinton publicly praised Stephen Carter's pro–free exercise book *The Culture of Disbelief.* President Kennedy, commenting on the *Engel* decision, used the occasion to urge people to pray privately. Most modern presidents do not appear to have placed a high priority on issues involving church-state separation. Rather, they have typically made statements that generally favor religion while avoiding the controversy associated with particular church-state issues.

It is perhaps ironic that the most explicit support for religious separatism has come from presidents whose religious identities have been in some sense distinctive. President Kennedy, whose Catholicism was something of an electoral liability (Converse 1966), did support the *Engel* decision, albeit with a notable lack of enthusiasm. Similarly, Jimmy Carter, whose credentials as a "born-again" Christian constituted a moderately important issue in the presidential campaign of 1976, adopted an explicitly separatist position on school prayer (which he modified after becoming president). This suggests that presidents who are strongly identified with a *specific* denomination or religious tradition have been particularly wary of endorsing religious accommodationism, for fear of alienating potential supporters from outside their faith.[9]

One prominent exception was President Ronald Reagan. Reagan, elected with the support of several leaders of the Christian right, invoked religious imagery rather frequently in order to express opposition to abortion and support for school prayer. Reagan frequently spoke out in favor of school prayer, and of religion in general, citing the intentions of the "Founding Fathers" as support for his views. "If we could get government out of the classroom," Reagan is quoted as saying, "maybe we could get God back in" (Moen 1990). In 1982, Reagan submitted a school prayer amendment to Congress, but the amendment was not passed. Several analysts have suggested that even Reagan, who was perhaps the most publicly "pro-religion" president in modern times, gave only passive and rhetorical support to religious accommodation or free exercise.

It is not entirely clear why there has been so little activity in the area of church-state relations on the part of the U.S. government's chief executive. It may simply be that presidents seek to husband their limited political capital and avoid the controversy that active engagement in issues such as school prayer or tuition tax credits might entail. Presidents have had the option of deferring publicly either to state and local governments (where most contemporary church-state issues are contested) or to the Supreme Court. It might also be that demographic groups generally opposed to religious accommodation (members of minority religions, or recent immigrants) tend to be concentrated in large, urban areas rich in electoral votes. Catholics and Jews, historically most numerous in heavily populated, urban states, have typically been quite skeptical of public accommodation to what might be regarded as a Protestant majority. The logic of presidential selection might be operating in favor of a passive presidential role in church-state relations (Burns 1963). The same public opinion that incites some members of Congress to raise issues of church-state separation may provide disincentives for presidents or presidential candidates to place such issues on the public agenda. Although presidents often maintain liaisons with religious interest groups (Hertzke 1989), it is unusual for the U.S. chief executive to take a leadership role in controversies involving church-stare relations.

Similarly, issues relating to religious establishment or free exercise have received little attention from the federal bureaucracy. Given the preeminence of the courts in such matters and the general unpopularity of the Supreme Court's separatist decisions, there has been little interest among government bureaucrats either in enforcing or in defying the Court's edicts at the level of policy implementation. One prominent set of exceptions emerged during the Reagan administration: Solicitor General Rex Lee submitted *amicus curiae* briefs in a number of court cases, supporting religious accommodationism in issues involving the constitutionality of state legislative chaplains, publicly sponsored Nativity scenes, school prayer, and aid to parochial schools (Murley 1988). Cabinet officials from the Departments of Justice and Education testified before Congress in favor of the school prayer amendment submitted by the Reagan administration. Note that even here, the activity of the executive branch was essentially reactive to decisions of the U.S. Supreme Court.

Occasionally, the Internal Revenue Service has been active in the area of church-state relations. Religious organizations traditionally have been exempted from federal taxes under the Free Exercise Clause. However, in at least one instance—that involving Bob Jones University—the IRS revoked a religious tax exemption because the institution had an official policy of racial discrimination (*Bob Jones University v. United States* [1983]). The university argued (unsuccessfully) that the Free Exercise Clause provided an exemption from federally mandated rules against racial discrimination.

As noted above, the law likewise places strict limitations on the political activities of tax-exempt organizations. Several religious organizations (including the USCC) appear to have voluntarily limited their participation in politics as a result of this policy (Fauser et al. 1995). However, there have been relatively few instances of a tax exemption being revoked due to an organization's inappropriate political activity.

In sum, the involvement of the federal bureaucracy in issues of church-state relations has been limited. The powers even of popularly elected federal officials to make policy in this area are circumscribed; and lacking any institutional incentive for such activity, agencies of the federal executive branch have typically remained passive with regard to issues of religious free exercise or establishment. Given that presidents have few incentives to intervene directly in church-state relations, they are unlikely to provide much guidance to appointed officials.

Conclusion

There is only a weak correspondence between public opinion and public policy on issues of church-state relations. Public opinion is supportive of church-state separation in the abstract, but generally supports the accommodation of religious belief in specific cases. Nevertheless, public policy on the whole has been separatist with respect to issues involving the Establishment Clause.

The continuing disparity between public opinion and policy regarding church-state relations can be attributed to two factors: Firstly, even in the presence of high levels of popular support, it has proven difficult to challenge the prevailing legal interpretations of the Establishment Clause. Secondly, the existence of different, overlapping constituencies within American politics, and the accountability of elected officials to these aggregations of citizens, keep the question of church-state relations on the public agenda and prevent any definitive resolution. As long as state and (especially) local governments enjoy a degree of autonomy on issues such as public education, it will be in the interests of some elected officials to press the limits of the Supreme Court's separatism in order to satisfy public opinion in areas in which accommodationism is particularly popular. The same incentive seems likely to motivate the behavior of some incumbent or prospective members of the House of Representatives. However, national elites (such as presidents or presidential aspirants) may find it expedient to deemphasize the political aspects of religious belief and practice.

In recent years, accommodationists have begun to utilize a powerful legal and rhetorical weapon in the conflict over the public role of religion: the Free Exercise Clause. Despite the Court's rulings in *Smith* and *Boerne,* religious elites have shifted their focus from narrowing the Establishment Clause to focusing on questions of religious liberty. This shift to greater correspondence with the American tradition of individualism is the subject of the next chapter.

Questions for Discussion

1. Why has Congress pursued accommodationist or libertarian policies in the face of adverse Supreme Court rulings? Is the continuation of the church-state debate desirable in terms of its effects on American democracy?

2. Is the dominance of the Supreme Court in policymaking in the church-state area consistent with your understanding of democracy? How might things be different?

3. Do the IRS restrictions on the political activities of tax-exempt organizations violate the free exercise rights of such groups? Their free speech rights?

4. Why are presidents typically so passive in the area of church-state relations? Might it make more sense for some future president to act as a moral leader by taking a firm position on these issues? How might such a position affect a president's ability to govern?

Notes

1. This section summarizes results reported more fully in Jelen and Wilcox 1995.

2. It may be instructive to read Justice John Stewart's dissent in *Engel v. Vitale,* or Justice Antonin Scalia's dissent in *Board of Education of Kiryas Joel Village School District v. Grumet* (see Biskupic 1994; Greenhouse 1994). Both of these opinions defend religious accommodationism from the standpoint of preserving religious free exercise.

3. For a more detailed analysis of religious issues related to conscientious objection, see Pfeffer (1967) and Choper (1995).

4. In a concurring opinion, Justice Sandra Day O'Connor suggested that compelling state interest was in fact the appropriate standard in free exercise cases, and that the gov-

ernment had met its burden of proof in *Smith*. In a dissenting opinion, Justice Blackmun argued that although the compelling state interest standard was the correct one, the state of Oregon had not met its burden of proof.

5. An "easy" issue is one that does not require the citizen to have a great deal of contextual information in order to have an opinion. "Easy" issues typically have been on the political agenda for a long time, deal with ends rather than means, and have strong symbolic value.

6. For a more complete overview of the legislative history of the school prayer issue, see Murley (1988).

7. Predicting the actions of the Supreme Court is a hazardous enterprise; but I suspect that the RLPA will fare no better than the RFRA, if and when the measure receives judicial scrutiny. The Court has recently appeared willing to limit the authority of Congress under the Commerce Clause, as it did in *U.S. v. Lopez* (1995).

8. If a proposed constitutional amendment passes both the U.S. House and Senate with a two-thirds majority, it must then be ratified by three-fourths of the state legislatures.

9. Most observers would agree that there were important differences in the personal religiosity of Kennedy and Carter. Nevertheless, both were identified with particular religious traditions.

4

·····································

From Christian America
to Free Exercise

*The Changing Nature of the
Church-State Debate*

A Hare Krishna solicits support from a passerby. The protection of religious liberty some-times entails inconvenience. (Photo © Owen Franken/Stock Boston)

T his chapter focuses on the contents of the arguments employed by the protagonists in the church-state debate. Activists who favor a vigorous religious presence in American politics have altered the justifications they offer for such a position. During the past two decades or so, proponents of religious accommodationism have switched their emphasis from a narrow, nonpreferentialist reading of the Establishment Clause to a libertarian understanding of the Free Exercise Clause. That is, rather than directing attention to the presumed constitutional power of government to offer neutral assistance to religion, religious conservatives have begun to focus on the religious prerogatives of individual citizens. Recent proponents of an assertive public religious presence have, in terms of the typology offered in Chapter 1, changed from a position of Christian preferentialism to one of religious nonpreferentialism. In keeping with this shift, the content of their argumentation has changed from legal or constitutional analysis, or a description of the incentives and constraints experienced by various political participants, to a discussion of normative conceptions of democratic government. The focus of such arguments is the relationship between the demands of religious discipleship and belief and those of democratic citizenship.

First, we will examine two common justifications for the assertion of religious values in political discourse: (1) that religion provides social cohesion, and (2) that it contributes significantly to individual liberty. Although there appears to be a general consensus on the symbolic value of the concept of "separation of church and state," there is no clear agreement on the precise meaning of the phrase. A "weak" sense of church-state separation can be justified on collective grounds of a common interest, or on the basis of defending individual liberty and autonomy. I begin by exploring the normative dimensions of these arguments about the role religion *should* play in democratic politics. Second, I argue that although elements of both system-level and individual-level arguments have always been present in public discourse about church-state relations, arguments for politically assertive religion have shifted from claims of how religion might serve a general, public interest to how religion serves to protect individual freedom and empower individual citizens. I describe and examine a change in the rhetoric (defined here simply as persuasive speech) concerning the role religion plays in American political life.

These foci are connected in part because of the multicultural character of social and political life in the United States. As I argue later in this chapter, there is no consensus on either religion or morality in contemporary America. Therefore, religious activists have (perhaps unfairly) been denied some of their strongest arguments: the truth claims advanced by adherents of their religious traditions. Even if Christianity were a monolithic cultural force in the United States (a *very* implausible assumption), the large and growing presence of citizens who are members of religious traditions other than Christianity, and the existence of a large, visible secular population, render direct theological or moral appeals normatively inappropriate and politically ineffective. Therefore, apologists for religious accommodationism, or for a strong version of religious liberty, are forced to justify their arguments on political rather than religious grounds.

Dimensions of Democratic Discourse

In order to analyze the various arguments regarding the appropriate role of religion in a democracy, it is helpful to consider briefly some characteristics of democratic politics. Although many observers have identified "democracy" with a set of institutional arrangements (e.g., selection of public officials through elections, a free press, competitive political parties), my focus here is on the qualities of democratic discourse or deliberation—that is, on the nature of decisionmaking in a democratic system. I do not wish to suggest that the criteria I describe in this section are sufficient to label a political system "democratic," but only that the requisites listed below are *necessary* for democracy to be realized.

At its simplest level, *democracy* refers to a system of self-government—literally, "government by the people." Democracy is above all a system of governance, which means that decisions and policies made by democracies (as by other governments) are both authoritative and public. By *authoritative*, I mean that decisions are enforceable with the coercive, physical power of the state. Thus, although I may feel a moral obligation or duty to contribute to the United Way or the Juvenile Diabetes Foundation, this "obligation" is different from the obligation to pay income taxes to the federal government. I might experience a sense of moral guilt if I fail to contribute to charity; but the consequences of such a failure are vastly dissimilar from those associated with failure to pay taxes. Presumably, the former omission will not result in jail time, whereas the latter might well result in a loss of income or of physical freedom. In the final analysis, one cannot "agree to differ" with government authorities. One must typically comply with government edicts or risk suffering very tangible consequences.

The *public* nature of democratic governance means simply that laws are, in principle, applied to all citizens covered by particular regulations. Governments routinely make distinctions among citizens on the basis of age, income, or histories of criminal activity; but the notion of "equal protection" under the law means that governments may not discriminate among citizens who fall within a particular legally defined classification. Thus, democracy has as its primary concern the formulation and enforcement of policies of general applicability.

Because democracy is a system of *self*-governance, the preferences and values of *private* citizens are a matter of *public* concern. One could, in principle, govern oneself without reference to external authority or coercion. However, since democratic governance involves public policies applicable to citizens generally, the notion of "self-governance" seems somehow paradoxical. Clearly, it might frequently be the case that democratic citizens will be compelled to comply with policies with which they disagree, or incur the penalties for noncompliance. One must generally obey the law, whether the regulation in question seems reasonable or not. Indeed, the nonvoluntary nature of compliance with law is arguably an essential feature of government in any form. Doing justice to the idea of democracy as self-governance requires that citizens have the opportunity to participate in the making of laws to which they will be subject. Whether it occurs in town meetings (via so-called direct democracy), referenda, or competitive elections to public office, citizen involvement is an essential component of democratic politics.

Unless a society is extremely homogeneous, it is not easy to reach a majority consensus. What the existence of real or potential conflict among democratic citizens means is that democracy is a *persuasive* system, in which people who seek office, or who seek to promote particular policies, are required to persuade their cocitizens of their fitness for office, or of the desirability of their policy proposals (Thiemann 1996). Although it would seem unreasonable to require that all citizens unanimously consent to all policies (but see Buchanan and Tullock 1962), the task of governing a society characterized by even minimal levels of diversity requires a public discourse designed to persuade sufficient numbers of people to empower the mobilization of government power. Thus, political candidates (including incumbents) often seek to increase their popularity, and interest groups seek to present their policy preferences (and themselves) in the most favorable light possible. Richard Neustadt's (1991) classic description of presidential power as "the power to persuade" is equally applicable to that of political activists in democratic systems.

Persuasion, in turn, requires the existence or discovery of a commonly shared set of values or beliefs. In order to persuade another person to agree with my position on a particular question, I must at some point locate a premise or assumption on which we can agree. Absent such a premise (what Stephen Toulmin [1974] has called a "warrant"), persuasion and agreement are probably impossible. For example, as a university professor, I have frequent occasion to counsel underachieving students to put more effort into their academic work. Such attempts at persuasion on my part typically involve making students aware of the consequences of poor grades (e.g., loss of financial aid, reduced opportunities for postgraduate study) or challenging certain assumptions students hold. Student may believe that they are incapable of doing the work ("I'm not very smart, so any extra effort will be wasted") or that the system of evaluation is illegitimate ("The professor has it in for me, so it doesn't matter how well I do"). The truth and falsity of these beliefs may offer a basis for discussion, *provided* that the students and I share the value judgment that higher grades are preferable to lower ones. If this common ground somehow does not exist ("I hate school, and I'm only here because my parents have forced me to be here. I'm trying to flunk out"), my efforts at persuasion are likely to be futile. Indeed, unless I am willing to initiate a discussion about the general value of higher education, this hypothetical student and I have no basis for further conversation.

In social interactions between private individuals, the failure to find a basis for persuasion or agreement is not necessarily problematic. We have the option simply to "agree to differ." In the example used in the preceding paragraph, I would have nothing to say to students determined to fail except to wish them well in those endeavors at which they hope to succeed. However, political persuasion is of a different order. Since the results of public deliberation are both public and authoritative, the choice of "agreeing to disagree" is not often available. The obligations of citizenship, unlike those of friendship or discipleship, are not typically optional. Because of the authoritative nature of political decisions, it is of cardinal importance that there be generally shared premises or warrants on which government policies can be justified. Absent such a set of commonly held beliefs, government typically has no alternative to coercion, which is inconsistent with the definition of democracy as self-government. Various analysts of democratic political discourse (Greenawalt 1988; Audi 1989; Perry 1991) have identified the requirement that authoritative warrants be commonly accepted, or "publicly accessible."

The requirement of **public accessibility** is perhaps best illustrated by a negative example: In 1981, James Watt was nominated by President Reagan to be his secretary of the interior. Watt was well known as a strong advocate of converting public lands to private use and developing wilderness areas for industrial purposes. At his confirmation hearings in the U.S. Senate, Watt was asked whether he felt an obligation to preserve the environment for future generations. Watt responded to this question by observing that a number of the predictions in the biblical book of Revelations appeared to be coming to pass. The apparent accuracy of these predictions led Watt to believe that the end of the world, as foretold in Revelations, was imminent. Therefore, Watt argued, there was no compelling reason to preserve natural resources for future generations, since it seemed entirely possible that relatively few future citizens would exist.

Clearly, Watt's right to free religious exercise permits him to believe in a form of dispensationalist theology and to derive his policy preferences from those beliefs. However, the use of such a narrowly theological argument is not an adequate public warrant for a prospective cabinet officer. Watt's expressed belief in a particular view of the Bible (on which his policy recommendations theoretically depended) was not sufficiently widespread to serve as a basis for political persuasion. The theology of premillennial dispensationalism does not provide a set of shared premises from which citizens can derive preferences or from which government officials can seek public support. Watt's very response to this question, one might argue, was a way of dismissing the questioner rather than a serious effort to persuade.

The search for common ground is often elusive in a diverse, multicultural society such as that of the United States. It is often argued that the importance we attach to political processes constitutes the shared cultural premise necessary for democratic governance (see Rawls 1993). That is, even though we may disagree vigorously about the desirability of particular political outcomes, it is of utmost importance that we agree on the legitimacy of the procedures by which these outcomes were created. For example, many of my friends were outraged at the failure of the U.S. Senate to remove President Clinton from office in 1999 after he had been impeached by the House of Representatives. Yet even though they regarded Clinton as morally and ethically unfit to serve as president, virtually all agreed that the failure of the Senate to convict Clinton on any count of impeachment by the two-thirds majority required by the Constitution meant that Clinton was legally entitled to complete his term. My attempts to persuade my Republican friends of Clinton's fitness for office were mysteriously unpersuasive (I considered myself a critical supporter of the president); but we did agree on the legitimacy of the impeachment procedure and on its unambiguous outcome.

Attitudes like these are so commonly held that we often forget how extraordinary it is that our commitment to the process often supersedes our support for, or opposition to, particular results. Indeed, one reason why public education is considered so important is that governments at all levels tend to believe that the inculcation of the civic basis of political legitimacy is crucial to effective governance. The curricula of most public elementary schools, junior and senior high schools, and state universities in the United States include heavy doses of U.S. history, civics, government, and constitutional understanding. One important purpose of such requirements (aside from keeping me employed) is the development of civic support for the political system, even when the costs of citizenship seem relatively high. To reiterate: Collective self-governance requires persuasion, and persuasion in turn requires the existence of commonly held areas of agreement. The creation and maintenance of publicly accessible warrants is an essential feature of democratic political systems.

Also involved in the idea of democracy as self-governance is the idea that public preferences must be translated into public policy. However, most analysts argue that the preferences held by individual citizens must be "authentic" (see Berman 1970), and not subject to coercion or undue manipulation (Dahl 1956), in order for genuine self-government to occur. For example, if I tell a class of students (to whom I will eventually assign grades) that the election of Candidate Smith over Candidate Jones will result in every student's grade being lowered by one letter (e.g., all A's will become B's), in an effort to encourage them to vote for Jones, it is likely that their preferences for Jones will be genuine, and perhaps intense as well. My admonition is not, strictly speaking, coercion, since I have no way of knowing which student voted for which candidate, and the votes of my students alone are unlikely to affect the outcome of the election. Furthermore, assuming the election occurs early enough in the school term, students have the option of dropping the course. However, the apparent availability of such choices would not justify my attempt to persuade students to vote for the candidate of my choice. Most of us, I believe, would object to this mode of persuasion on the grounds that students were not free to make unencumbered choices, or to act on those choices in the voting booth. The use of my professorial authority in this way would be an abuse of the power conferred upon me by the university.

This point can be generalized, and stated more formally. If the idea of democracy as self-governance is to be taken seriously, citizens must have the capacity to make unencumbered choices and to act on those choices within the set of legally and constitutionally defined institutions. Moreover, democratic citizens have the right of **self-determination**; that is, the right to participate in the formation of their own preferences or characters. To some extent, all of us are products of our upbringings, our educational experiences, and our environments. Each of us is exposed to a wide variety of social and intellectual influences, which together affect our values, beliefs, and preferences.[1] The citizen's right to self-determination simply involves an assertion that people must be allowed to take an active role in the formation of their experiences and environments, if their preferences are to be considered authentic.

Examples in point: As a liberal Democrat, I am much more likely to read (and to spend money on) left-of-center publications such as the *New Republic* or the *Nation* than conservative outlets such as the *National Review* or the *American Spectator*. It seems likely that this sort of selective exposure to print media will cause my initial beliefs to be reinforced and will minimize my exposure to perspectives that challenge my assumptions. Although I might justifiably be criticized for voluntarily limiting the range of arguments to which I am exposed, few people would deny me the right to read (or to refrain from reading) the publications I choose. This implies that I am entitled, as a self-governing citizen, to act on preferences that will affect the formation of my future preferences. More generally, as an agent capable of self-governance, I must be allowed to participate in the formation of my own character.

To take a more specifically religious example, my right to religious free exercise would, at a minimum, permit me to switch my denominational affiliation from Roman Catholic to Southern Baptist if I so chose. Such a change, if accompanied by regular attendance at religious services, would allow me to experience an entirely different range of judgments and beliefs about things moral and religious. This sort of environmental self-selection might have profound implications for my behavior as a consumer, a voter, a husband, or a parent, and might well affect the lives of a great many people with whom I have contact. My hypothetical conversion to the Baptist church seems likely to have consequences for my beliefs and values that I do not, or could not, anticipate. Nevertheless, it would be very difficult indeed to argue that such a voluntary conversion should in any way be limited or controlled by public authorities.

Indeed, it might well be argued that the mixed set of freedoms listed in the First Amendment to the Constitution have in common their importance in the self-directed formation of character. The freedoms of speech, press, assembly (and perhaps, of association), and religion seem to converge on the notion that the formation of a "self," as citizen, believer, or family member, is a process in which the individual is entitled to take an active role. Although it is certainly true that we are to some unknowable extent products of our environments, we attain a certain level of freedom by consciously choosing and shaping the circumstances that will, reciprocally, influence who and what each of us becomes (Sezer 1995).

Thus, as a system of governance, democracy requires the ability to mobilize the coercive powers of government in order to implement collective decisions. In addition, as a system in which the "self," or individual, figures prominently, democracy requires that citizens be persuaded of the legitimacy of the public decision-making process, and entitles ordinary citizens to a high level of individual autonomy and sovereignty.

What, then, does any of this have to do with the political role of religion? During the last third of the twentieth century, the United States witnessed a substantial increase in publicly visible political advocacy on the part of religiously motivated individuals and groups. If the term *rhetoric* is understood neutrally to refer to persuasive speech and writing, I will show in this chapter that the contemporary Christian Right has undergone a major transformation in its rhetorical strategy. In the earlier manifestations of the Religious Right (approximately corresponding to the decade of the 1980s), leaders such as Jerry Falwell, representing groups such as Moral Majority, emphasized the importance of religion as a source of *governing* values. That is, religious values were considered a major portion of the common values on which democratic governance ultimately depends. By contrast, more recent manifestations of the Christian Right (in general, a phenomenon of the 1990s), exemplars of which might include Christian Coalition and its former executive director, Ralph Reed, have justified the assertion of religious values in political life by emphasizing the importance of individual religious liberty. In sum, where the earlier Christian Right rhetoric focused on religion as essential to the democratic task of self-*governance,* the discourse in more recent periods has given priority to the religious *self,* that is, the citizen who is to govern and to be governed.

A Christian America?

In the late 1970s and early 1980s, the Christian Right, or the Religious Right, was advanced in part through religious television. Programs such as Jerry Falwell's *Old Time Gospel Hour,* Pat Robertson's *700 Club,* and Jim and Tammy Bakker's *PTL Club* were the most famous of a large number of programs that provided religious (usually conservative Christian) perspectives on contemporary politics. A number of political organizations were also formed with the intention of placing "morality" on the political agenda. Jerry Falwell's organization, Moral Majority, Inc., was perhaps the most famous and visible of these. Falwell claimed partial credit for Ronald Reagan's victory in the presidential election of 1980, and was credited with (or blamed for) the defeat of several prominent liberal Democrats in other elections that same year (Lipset and Raab 1981).

The Christian Right of the early 1980s justified its political activity in several different ways. Considerations of religious free exercise were never far from the consciousness of the leaders of the Christian Right; but Christian Right activists and their apologists tended to argue from the perspective of the necessity of publicly accessible warrants for government decisions. It was often argued that adherence to simple procedural norms of democracy was not sufficient to ensure political stability or popular support for government actions. It is, of course, not at all inconceivable that democratic means can be used to attain undemocratic ends. Americans, for example, are often reminded that Germans freely chose to be governed by Adolf Hitler through perhaps the most "democratic" electoral institutions ever devised. Rather, supporters of a politically assertive Christianity suggested the need for a consensus on a substantive conception of personal and social morality. Put more simply, democratic self-governance is difficult or impossible unless most people agree on a definition of right and wrong. Some sense of the limits within which the *content* of public policy can be debated, as well as agreement on the procedural requirements for democracy, are thought to be necessary to the conduct of democratic politics.

Religious conservatives during the early 1980s tended to argue that Christianity, or, more broadly, a "Judeo-Christian tradition" provided just such a set of publicly accessible premises. This argument, which took various forms (described below), was based on a factual claim: namely, that American citizens who were exercising their religious freedom would in fact reach a general agreement on the essentials of moral conduct. This agreement, in turn, provided a large but bounded space within which democratic politics could be conducted.

This idea is not new. Prior to the Civil War, Alexis de Tocqueville, in his classic work *Democracy in America,* commented on the emergence of a moral consensus within the religious pluralism of the United States:

> The sects that exist in the United States are innumerable. They all differ in respect to the worship which is due the Creator, but they all agree in respect to the duties which are due from man to man. . . . Moreover, all the sects of the United States are comprised within the great unity of Christianity, and *Christian morality is everywhere the same.* . . . Christianity, therefore, reigns without obstacle, by universal consent; the consequence is . . . that every principle of the moral world is fixed and determinate, although the political world is abandoned to the debates and experiments of men. (Tocqueville 1945, 314–315; emphasis added)

Tocqueville suggests that religious differences in the United States were confined to matters of doctrine and worship ("the worship due the Creator"), and the ethical implications of a generally shared Christianity were virtually universal. In politics, certain policy alternatives are not considered, because they are quite literally unthinkable in a society in which a moral consensus is observed. For Tocqueville, the "debates and experiments" of politics are conducted *within* a "fixed and determinate" moral context.

Tocqueville's argument, of course, implies that there are substantial limits to the religious diversity that a democratic republic such as the United States can withstand. Tocqueville's positive evaluation of the political role of religion in the

United States was based on an empirical claim: namely, that the ethical implications of the religions practiced in the United States were quite similar, and religious differences were primarily theological in nature. Placing these observations in a more modern context, we can conclude that although a Catholic might oppose abortion as a violation of natural law derived through reason, and an evangelical Protestant may take a "pro-life" position based on a close reading of biblical references in Exodus, Psalms, and the Song of Solomon (see Cook, Jelen, and Wilcox 1992; Jelen 1993), for Tocqueville (and for contemporary accommodationists) the most important fact would be the consensus between the two—that legal abortion should be restricted, if not eliminated.

Echoes of Tocqueville's argument can be heard in contemporary accommodationist readings of the Establishment Clause. But although the argument that a common religious frame of reference is important to the practice of American politics has been made rather frequently, the precise reasons for viewing a religious consensus as desirable have varied. For example, in his early work *Listen, America!*, Jerry Falwell (founder of Moral Majority) suggested that God may make collective judgments about the corruption or righteousness of entire nations. Matters that at first glance seem confined to the sphere of private morality, in this analysis, have important public consequences:

> Psalm 9:17 admonishes, "The wicked shall be turned into hell, and all the nations that forget God." America will be no exception. If she forgets God, she too will face His wrath and judgment like every other nation in the history of humanity. But we have the promise in Psalm 33:12, which declares, "Blessed is the nation whose God is the LORD." When a nation's ways please the Lord, that nation is blessed with supernatural help. (Falwell 1980, 24; emphasis in original)

In this passage, Falwell makes an explicitly theological claim, asserting that the morality of the entire nation provides a basis for divine favor or disfavor. In so doing, Falwell specifically invokes accounts from the Old Testament in which the nation of Israel declines or prospers according to the extent of its compliance with its "covenant" with God.

Clearly, acceptance of Falwell's argument concerning the importance of morality and religion to the public life of the nation depends on one's acceptance of a particular set of theological warrants. Reichley identifies the Judeo-Christian tradition with an ethical system he describes as "theist-humanism." After a careful comparison of this set of beliefs with a variety of alternatives, he asserts the superiority of the Judeo-Christian perspective: "Theist-humanism solves the problem of balancing individual rights against social authority by rooting both in God's transcendent purpose, which is concerned for the welfare of each human soul.

But it does create a body of shared values through which problems can be mediated" (Reichley 1985, 52).

Tocqueville located the public consensus that religion provides at the level of moral application. Commenting on the theological diversity of religion in the United States, he suggested that this diversity in fact resulted in agreement on principles of moral behavior. In contrast, Falwell's focus is squarely on what Tocqueville called "the duties owed the Creator." For Falwell, it is the relationship between God and humanity, rather than the relationship between humans, that mandates an assertive public role for religion.

Reichley appears to take an intermediate position between these two arguments. Unlike Falwell, Reichley is not committed to the truth value of specifically theological claims offered by religious leaders (although he is clearly sympathetic to such claims). What matters most, in Reichley's view, is not simply that Americans agree on particular prescriptions or proscriptions of moral behavior but that these ethical applications result from a belief system in which public authority and individual autonomy are both valued.

Richard Neuhaus also has echoed Tocqueville's call for the political necessity for a moral consensus:

> Politics derives its directions from the ethos, from the cultural sensibilities that are the context of political action. The cultural context is shaped by our moral judgments and intuitions about how the world is and how it ought to be. Again, for the great majority of Americans, such moral judgments and intuitions are inseparable from religious belief. (Neuhaus 1984, 137)

Neuhaus, like Tocqueville, has located the (presumably shared) "cultural sensibilities" of American political culture at the level of morality ("moral judgments and intuitions"). Like Tocqueville, Neuhaus also has suggested that there is a strong empirical connection between shared moral values and the religious beliefs held by ordinary Americans.

In sum, arguments that religion benefits democratic discourse vary substantially in their particulars: Falwell has asserted that public adherence to the tenets of a "Judeo-Christian tradition" are politically advantageous because such tenets are true. Reichley, although making no truth claims in behalf of Christianity, has suggested that shared values are generally desirable, and the tenets of this particular belief system are uniquely beneficial. Although personally sympathetic to Christianity, Tocqueville and Neuhaus both argued that the political value of religion lies in the extent to which such beliefs are generally shared.

However, these differences in argumentation should not obscure an important similarity, which in my view provides the basis for an accommodationist reading of the Establishment Clause: Religion (singular) is ultimately good for democratic politics, because a *shared* adherence to a common religious tradition provides a set of publicly accessible assumptions within which democratic politics can be conducted. Absent such shared values, it is suggested, democracy as a system of *self*-governance that relies on persuasion is impossible, and politics is reduced to raw competition between selfish people with highly unequal levels of political power.

This argument has several important implications: First, the notion that religious values provide the context for democratic deliberation suggests the desirability of a narrow, nonpreferentialist reading of the Establishment Clause emphasizing the presumed beneficial consequences of religion. Government at all levels *ought* to provide nondiscriminatory aid to religious bodies, because the public affirmation of religious belief and practice generally has positive consequences for secular political life. Second, if religion in general is a source of social or political cohesion, then there is no necessary tension between the religion clauses of the First Amendment. The assumption of a shared national religious heritage implies that individual citizens, freely exercising their religious beliefs, will produce something approaching a moral or ethical consensus. If there is general agreement on the essentials of a Judeo-Christian tradition, then it is unlikely that the ethical consequences of religion will produce much cultural conflict. An active, benevolent neutrality toward religion is thus the appropriate stance for government.

Lastly, the assumption that cultural consensus is based on common religious values implies that there is no necessary tension between religion and democracy. If citizens who share a culture of common religious assumptions engage in self-determination, and participate in public affairs, the result seems likely to satisfy the requisites of democratic self-governance (public acceptance of government authority; popular persuasion; and the translation of authentic public preferences into public policy), as well as the requisites of a shared, religiously based public morality. If the empirical claim of moral consensus in a Judeo-Christian nation is in fact correct, the demands of political citizenship and religious discipleship seem likely to be compatible rather than contradictory. If such a consensus in fact exists, there is likely to be a congruence between individual preferences and the public, collective demands of democratic governance.

If this generally benevolent description of the relationship between religion and politics in early America is accurate, what went wrong? How is it that religion has come to be a source of conflict in contemporary American politics, and how is it that the Supreme Court has generally endorsed a separatist reading of the Establishment Clause? If there is in fact general agreement concerning the religious/moral foundation of American politics, why is the Christian Right even necessary?

According to apologists for the Christian Right, the answer to this question is that the purported agreement over fundamental principles of religion and morality is not quite complete. Indeed, members of the Christian Right often argue that a small but politically powerful minority of Americans has succeeded in enforcing an undemocratic, un-Christian political agenda. This minority consists of privileged persons who are irreligious and hostile to the moral values held by most Americans (Rusher 1988). Such persons tend to be employed in the news or entertainment media or in academic institutions, which provide them extraordinarily powerful forums in which to promote their secular agendas. Unlike elected officials, these individuals are not accountable to anyone. This liberal, "verbalist" class (Rusher 1988; Hunter 1980) has a disproportionate influence over the political process. According to the Christian Right, it is no accident that the immediate source of separatist policies has been the Supreme Court, which is (as I noted in the second chapter of this book) the branch of government least accountable to public opinion. To the extent that secular elites wield political influence in American politics, the process is considered undemocratic, and the resulting policies, un-Christian.

According to some accommodationist analysts, the creed of the secular elite is humanism, a loosely constructed ideology that is presented as an enlightened alternative to more traditional sources of morality. As Jerry Falwell has written:

> Humanism claims a "life adjustment" philosophy. The emphasis is placed on a person's social and psychological growth instead of on factual knowledge. "Socialization" has become the main purpose of education. Students are told that there are no absolutes and that they are to develop their own value systems. The humanist creed is documented in two humanist manifestos, signed in 1933 and 1973. Humanists believe that man is his own god and that moral values are relative, that ethics are situational. Humanists say that the Ten Commandments and other moral and ethical laws are "outmoded" and hindrances to human progress. Humanism places man at the center of the universe. . . . It teaches that man is not a unique and specific creation of God. Man is merely the ultimate product of the evolutionary process who has gained a sense of intelligence that prevents him from acting like an animal. (Falwell 1980, 206)

In his dissenting opinion in *Edwards v. Aguillard*, Justice Scalia also made reference to the dominance of "secular humanism" in public education. Many other religious conservatives also view humanism as exerting a disproportionate and illegitimate influence on the processes and policies of American politics. The name *Moral Majority* symbolizes the beliefs that religious accommodationism and political democracy are compatible and that the ascendancy of separatism is the re-

sult of a distortion of the process of popular governance. If politics were more democratic, it is often argued, the government would be more supportive of the
public expression of religious belief.

By most accounts, this tendency in religious politics in the United States has
not been particularly successful, nor have its arguments persuaded either the
courts or public opinion (see Wilcox 1996). Groups such as Moral Majority failed
to attract more than a small fraction of their potential constituencies (Buell and
Sigelman 1985, 1987; Sigelman, Wilcox, and Buell 1987; Wilcox 1987, 1992; Jelen
1991). The presidential campaign of televangelist Marion "Pat" Robertson gar-
nered only weak support, even among his most likely constituents (Green 1995;
Jelen 1993).

The apparent failure of the older, 1980s version of the Christian Right seems
to have had a number of different causes. Firstly, the movement was divided in-
ternally by the effects of religious particularism (Glock and Stark 1968)—a belief
in the superiority of a narrowly defined religious tradition. In the 1980s, cooperation between groups of conservative Christians proved difficult, primarily due
to differences in religious doctrine. Despite Tocqueville's observation of a moral
consensus among American Christians, divisions between Catholics and Protestants (see Reed 1994) and between Protestant fundamentalists and Pentecostals
(Jelen 1991; Wilcox 1992) prevented the formation of large, multidenomina-
tional coalitions. For example, in 1988, Jerry Falwell did not endorse fellow televangelist Pat Robertson, but endorsed George Bush several months prior to the
primary season. Despite the fact that it was difficult to find *political* issues on
which Falwell and Robertson disagreed, Falwell was apparently repelled by
Robertson's "spirit-filled" brand of Christianity. Robertson claimed spiritual
gifts such as the ability to divert hurricanes, the gift of faith healing, and glosso-
lalia(speaking in tongues). Falwell's more austere brand of Protestant fundamentalism apparently led him to regard Robertson's theological positions as quite
implausible. Thus, contrary to Tocqueville's expectations, and to the arguments
made by proponents of nonpreferentialism, religious doctrine does in fact matter, and doctrinal differences among Christians obstructed the formation of
Christian political coalitions.

Secondly, public reaction to the Religious Right in the 1980s made the notion
of any moral consensus seem ludicrous, even apart from theological/ideological
disagreements. The increasingly common practices of extramarital sex, abortion,
and homosexuality threw fuel on already contentious public debates about
morality. If there is any general agreement among Americans today on questions
of morality, the content of such an agreement is difficult to discern. Nor can debates between "traditional" and "progressive" conceptions of morality (Hunter

1991) be reduced to disagreement between religious and irreligious citizens. Many Christian (primarily liberal Protestant) denominations have taken leadership roles in the promotion of nontraditional moral beliefs. For example, the leaders of one mainline Protestant denomination have advanced the concept of "justice-love," in which the morality of sexual relationships is to be evaluated by the power relationships between the participants rather than their gender or marital status (Ostling 1991). What matters most is whether such relationships are "exploitive" or "mutually supportive," and not whether physical bonding occurs within or outside the bounds of traditional marriage. Thus, it has become increasingly difficult to assert that there is anything approaching a consensus on issues of personal morality in the contemporary United States.

Garry Wills (1990) has argued that it only became necessary to assert publicly that America is a "Christian nation" when such a statement was no longer true. If indeed there were a religious and/or moral consensus in the United States, we would presumably take such values for granted, and it would be unnecessary to make such a consensus the subject of strident public commentary.

The lack of consensus over personal morality can, to a large extent, be attributed to a reassertion of the value of individualism. Even highly religious and highly conservative citizens have been repelled by the attempts of the Christian Right to "legislate morality," or to give their religious convictions the force of law. Evangelical Protestants who disapprove of feminism, homosexuality, or adultery are nonetheless able to distinguish between sins and crimes, and to assign responsibility for punishing the former to God.[2] Put in constitutional language, when moral values are contested, government enforcement of religious values may no longer be nonpreferential, and may instead violate the Establishment Clause.[3]

Some religious conservatives have revived Roger Williams's argument (described in Chapter 2) of a religious basis for separatism. These individuals regard the church's involvement in the secular world of politics as having a contaminating effect on the practice of authentic religion. In theological terms, identification of religious symbols with secular candidates, parties, or policies runs the risk of idolatry, by attributing divine characteristics to human products. For example, Glenn Tinder (1989) has argued that it is very un-Christian for believers to derive particular political messages from the Gospels. Tinder points out that unlike Old Testament works such as Exodus or Leviticus (which contain detailed lists of regulations and penalties), the Gospels of Matthew, Mark, Luke, and John are narratives describing the speech and actions of Jesus. When one of us presumes to make an authoritative statement about the political meaning of Christ's teachings, we are guilty of mixing material from a divine source (God's Word) with judgments derived from our fallible, corrupt, human reason. It is thus a very bad *theological* error to derive specific political meanings from religious sources. Identification of religious principles with political values can be considered a violation of the First Commandment as well as the First Amendment.

More generally, religious identification with particular political figures or causes has occasionally seemed counterproductive to the achievement of religiously defined moral goals. In 1980, groups such as Moral Majority encouraged evangelical Christians to vote, and took partial credit for Ronald Reagan's victory in the presidential election. In 1989, at the end of Reagan's term, abortion remained legal, organized prayer in public schools was still prohibited, and the larger part of the Moral Majority's legislative agenda remained unimplemented. Although evangelical Christians proved to be the Republican Party's most reliable bloc of voters during the 1980s (Kellstedt et al. 1994), conservative Christian support for the GOP did not result in a more visibly "Christian" set of public policies.

In sum, the assertion of values of religious accommodation during the 1980s was neither politically nor intellectually successful. Religious conservatives who sought a more visible, active role for religion in the public sphere did not witness major shifts in constitutional doctrine, nor did they see their preferences enacted as public policy. Moreover, the political conflict occasioned by the earlier manifestations of the Christian Right in the 1980s tended to call some of the factual assumptions underlying a narrow reading of the Establishment Clause into question. The contested nature of moral issues in the 1980s, and the failure of religious conservatives to attract public support for their agenda, suggested that claims of a religious, moral, or ethical consensus in American political life are quite implausible. Thus, given the framework of democratic discourse described earlier in this chapter, contemporary religion does not appear to provide a set of publicly accessible premises within which democratic politics can be conducted.[4]

A Place at the Table

In response to the apparent shortcomings of the "old" Christian Right, the focus of religious activists changed from religion as a source of support for self-*governance* to the *self* that is to be governed. More recent religious activism has undergone a shift in emphasis from questions of religious establishment—what government can legitimately do to provide nondiscriminatory assistance to religion—to an emphasis on questions of religious free exercise. Rather than focusing on the public benefits of religion as a source of social cohesion and integration, more recent proponents of an active political role for religion have suggested the need for greater religious autonomy and freedom.

Attention to the prerogatives associated with the Free Exercise Clause has always been an important component of the rhetoric of religious activists; but recently, the notion that religious freedom requires government deference to the public assertion of religious belief has become much more central to the efforts of religious conservatives. Indeed, the Christian Coalition, which is the most recent manifestation of the Religious Right, has specifically eschewed any notion of a "Christian America" in favor of a "place at the table" in public dialogue. It holds that a separatist reading of the Establishment Clause is problematic not because it undermines an important source of public morality but because it has caused unwarranted interference with the free exercise of religion.

In his 1993 book *The Culture of Disbelief* (which has been cited with approval by President Clinton), Stephen Carter argued that an overly rigid and narrow understanding of the separation of church and state has led to religion's being denied its rightful place in the public dialogue. The efforts of secular elites to purge public discourse of religious content has led to a situation in which religion is simply regarded as a "hobby," with no important public contributions or consequences. In a chapter entitled "The 'Christian Nation' and Other Horrors," Carter essentially dismissed the idea that the accommodation of religious belief leads to unconstitutional religious establishment: "Our secular politics is unlikely to become the servant of any single religious tradition; the nation has become too secure in its diversity to allow that travesty to occur. But it is quite possible for religion to become the servant of secular politics, and, in the 1980s, some would say, it nearly did" (Carter 1993, 97). Similar sentiments have been voiced by Ralph Reed, the former executive director of Christian Coalition:

> The movement is best understood as an essentially defensive struggle by people seeking to sustain their faith and their values. . . . Presumably all of us want freedom to practice our religion, to enjoy the rights of free speech guaranteed by the First Amendment, and to fully participate in our duties of citizenship. Yet intolerance towards religion has reached disturbing levels, threatening civility and undermining a basic sense of fairness. (Reed 1994, 18, 41)

According to these observers, church-state relations have become a contested area because of unwarranted government intrusion into the right of religious free exercise. In the language of the schoolyard, religious conservatives continue to assert the need for a strong public role for religion because "they [the government] started it."

This shift toward the language of Free Exercise is an important substantive and persuasive strategy. Questions of religious freedom, as opposed to the assertion of religiously based stands on moral issues, are consistent with the American value of individual liberty. Policies described as reasserting personal freedom seem to be much more easily accepted by Americans of differing types and levels of religious affiliation. American political rhetoric is often laced with what Mary Ann Glendon (1991) has termed "rights talk." The assertion of religious rights seems likely to be more persuasive than attempts to legislate morality.

Moreover, this renewed emphasis on the free exercise of religion benefits from the religious and moral diversity of American citizens. To the extent that pluralism precludes the likelihood of any publicly shared assumptions, it seems plausible to argue that religious values have a legitimate place in political discourse. As Kent Greenawalt (1988, 113) has argued:

> If commonly shared moral perspectives and forms of reason provide no evidently correct perspective, it is hard to understand why a liberal democrat should eschew his deeply held religious premises in favor of some alternative assumptions that also lie beyond public reasons and can yield a starting point. . . . Everyone must reach beyond commonly accessible reasons to decide many social issues, and . . . religious bases for such decisions should not be disfavored in comparison to other possible bases.

In this passage, Greenawalt has conceded that religion is unlikely to provide a common cognitive framework within which political discourse can be conducted. However, he also suggests that for many issues confronting a morally and religiously diverse citizenry, such publicly accessible warrants simply do not exist— whether within or outside of religious beliefs. Given that social issues must eventually be decided and that there is no clearly defined means for settling them, religiously based values have as much right to be presented as those derived from any other perspective.

Examples in point: In 1925, the "Scopes Monkey Trial" was contested in Tennessee. Scopes, a high school biology teacher, was tried for teaching the theory of evolution, which violated a Tennessee statute that prohibited the teaching of any account of the origins of the human species that was not consistent with the biblical account in Genesis (Wills 1990). As mentioned earlier in this chapter, evolution is considered by some religious conservatives to be a central tenet of secular humanism and to undermine faith in the inerrancy of the Bible. Although Scopes was convicted, he was fined only a token amount, and the Tennessee law was exposed to a good deal of public ridicule. Indeed, the entire fundamentalist movement lost a great deal of public credibility as a result of *Scopes*.[5]

In recent years, a number of religious conservatives have attempted to challenge the hegemony of evolutionary theory in biology curricula and to reinstate the teaching of creationism in public high schools. However, rather than argue that creationism should be taught exclusively, as the "correct" theory of human origins, legislatures in states such as Arkansas and Louisiana during the 1980s passed regulations mandating that equal time be given to both explanations. Both evolution and creationism would be taught as competing theories of natural history, with students being encouraged to make up their own minds. Some research has suggested that this "fairness" approach to the teaching of creationism is quite popular, even among citizens who are not necessarily sympathetic to a literal reading of the Bible (Martin and Jelen 1989). The argument here is that government, by enforcing the teaching of evolution (through compulsory public education and grading), is interfering with the religious free exercise rights of schoolchildren and their parents. At a minimum, the guarantee of religious freedom would seem to suggest that parents have the right to raise their children in the faith of their (parents') choice. If the system of public education, which parents are required to support, undermines that religious training, then the religious liberty of parents whose beliefs cause them to reject the theory of evolution is being violated by curricular decisions.

From the standpoint of political efficacy, the advantage of this approach is that religious conservatives (in this instance, creationists) need not persuade citizens with different religious beliefs of the correctness of their view of Scripture. Rather, all that is required is that cocitizens (and by extension, government) be convinced of the sincerity of the creationists' beliefs, *and* in the legal and ethical requirement that those beliefs be respected. To someone convinced of the literal correctness of the entire Bible, this might seem like "half a loaf"; but to most creationists, such a policy seems clearly preferable to one in which secular beliefs are disseminated and enforced without contradiction. However, my conversations with colleagues who teach biology suggest that many instructors faced with fundamentalist opposition have elected to forgo class discussion of the origins of the world altogether. Although equal time provisions offer an approach to the teaching of creationism that may be acceptable to many Americans with a wide range of religious beliefs, their use in concrete instances has been challenged and has not yet been upheld by the Supreme Court.

Similarly, religious activists and sympathetic state and local legislatures have attempted to chip away at the ban on school prayer established in *Engel v. Vitale*. Various subnational governments have permitted school districts to conduct "moments of silence" during which individual students may choose to pray, meditate, or (perhaps) admire the beautiful person in the next row. Other measures have permitted "voluntary," student-led prayer in public settings, such as at commencement ceremonies and athletic events. Certain recent court rulings have suggested that student-run religious publications can be funded on the same basis as other student publications and that religious groups may use public school facilities on the same basis as nonreligious organizations. That is, if the chess club or the National Honor Society is permitted to use classroom space after school hours, then student-initiated religious organizations cannot legally be denied the same privilege (*Lamb's Chapel v. Center Moriches Union Free School District,* 1993). In all of these cases, the principle involved is not the social or political desirability of the public assertion of religious belief but that of nondiscrimination. Contemporary religious conservatives such as Ralph Reed and Stephen Carter have plausibly suggested that it is inappropriate for government to single out religious ideas for special treatment. In this line of reasoning, it is not a violation of the Establishment Clause for government to offer benefits to religious organizations on the same basis as other groups.

What all this means, of course, is that the most important contribution religion is considered to make to the democratic process of self-governance is the enhancement of the citizen's capacity for self-determination. As many church-state issues involve questions of public education, religious claims against the authority of public schools may be regarded as limitations on the ability of government to engage in overt political socialization, and may provide alternative perspectives by which future citizens may engage in the formation of their own characters.

The focus of religious activists has thus been diverted from the role of religion as a source of *governmental* empowerment (by assisting in the legitimation of democratic decisionmaking) to one of *individual* empowerment. Religion benefits society by benefiting the development of individual citizens. Indeed, academic literature suggests that participation in religious organizations enhances the development of civic skills such as participation in group decisionmaking, compromise, and public speaking (Verba, Schlozman, and Brady 1995; Peterson 1992). Moreover, the findings of the research team led by Sidney Verba suggest that religion is in fact the *only* such empowering institution available to citizens who are otherwise (educationally, socially, and economically) disadvantaged. Unlike education, active involvement in other organizations, and high levels of discretionary income (which tend to provide political advantages to citizens who are already well-off), religious involvement tends to have a "Robin Hood" effect, assisting those who otherwise would lack political skills and resources.

The renewed attention that religious conservatives have devoted to religious free exercise has posed a strategic dilemma for some of the separatist groups described in Chapter 3. This point is raised with particular clarity by the different reactions of two groups classified as "free-marketeers"—the ACLU and PAW—to the Religious Liberty Protection Act (RLPA), recently introduced in Congress. As the word *free-marketeer* implies, these groups are committed to a separatist view of the Establishment Clause and a libertarian view of the Free Exercise Clause. Theoretically, both groups should favor a measure restoring a high level of religious deference to claims of religious free exercise. However, this has not been the case. The ACLU has opposed the RLPA on the basis of its possible use to exempt religiously motivated citizens from complying with laws proscribing discrimination. As an in-depth analysis on the ACLU Website noted:

> Passage of an unamended RLPA would have undermined many state and local civil rights laws by creating a new defense against civil rights claims brought under those laws. RLPA would particularly undermine many of those state and local laws which protect groups that get the least protection from the courts and the federal government, namely, disability, sexual orientation, familial status, marital status, pregnancy status, and possibly gender and religion. (ACLU 1999)

In contrast, in a Web message entitled "Why We Support the Religious Liberty Protection Act," People for the American Way took the opposite position:

> *The fear has arisen among some of our allies that RLPA will be used to claim an exemption from civil rights laws protecting gay men and lesbians. . . . If some people want to misuse religion as a defense against the violation of anti-discrimination laws, they can do so (as they have already) regardless of what happens with RLPA.* (PAW 1999; emphasis in original)

At stake is the question of whether certain forms of discrimination can be justified by claims of religious free exercise. Indeed, a religious justification for racial discrimination was the (unsuccessful) defense used in the 1983 *Bob Jones* case. If one's religious conviction requires one to avoid interaction with certain classes of people, is it not possible that government policies mandating such interaction violate the Free Exercise Clause?

For example, if a landlord believes that homosexuality or premarital sex is sinful, but lives in a state in which discrimination on the basis of sexual orientation or marital status is illegal, could the landlord legally refuse to rent to a gay couple or to an unmarried heterosexual couple on the basis of religious convictions? Some religious conservatives would argue that free religious exercise does provide a defense against legal actions motivated by alleged acts of discrimination. One's religiously based "right" to shun people who are guilty of sin may be regarded as more fundamental than the right of the "sinners" to continue to engage in immoral behavior. Conversely, allowing such exemptions from antidiscrimination laws would certainly limit the freedom of entire classes of people with respect to housing, employment, credit opportunities, and other prerogatives of individuals living in a free society.

It is not clear under RLPA whether acts of discrimination allegedly motivated by religious belief would supersede other rights, such as the right to freedom of association, which gay couples might claim, or an unmarried couple's right to privacy. Such questions admit of no easy resolution; and the rote adoption of a position in favor of "personal liberty" provides no meaningful guidance. Since RLPA's proponents in Congress claim to be interpreting a constitutional right authoritatively, it seems quite conceivable that claims of religious liberty might indeed "trump" other liberties guaranteed by the Bill of Rights, and that the fears of the ACLU may be well grounded. Yet it remains politically awkward for the ACLU, an organization whose sole purpose is the protection of civil liberties, to take a public position against religious freedom.

The recent emphasis on the politics of religious free exercise has led to a reconsideration of the public role of religion, spearheaded by religiously motivated political activists. Recall that earlier accounts of political religion drew attention to the consensual, integrative social function of religion. As Tocqueville eloquently put it, "Christianity rules by universal consent, and Christian morality is everywhere the same." For Falwell, Reichley, and Neuhaus, religion performs an essentially conservative function, providing a basis on which government regulations can be made and legitimately enforced. David Leege (1993) has termed this fusion of religious and governmental authority the "priestly" role of religion.

In contrast, current religious activists emphasize what might be considered a "prophetic" political use for religion. Rather than supplementing and enhancing the authority of government, religion is now described as a source of social and political criticism. The words of Ralph Reed illustrate this viewpoint:

> Today's religious reformers are often ridiculed and misunderstood. But so were previous social dissenters who operated in a religious context. . . . The antislavery crusade, temperance movement, and civil rights struggle all owed their distinctive moral flavor to the messianic zeal of their adherents. Religion sparking political involvement is not an aberration of the American experience, but is perhaps its most persistent theme. (Reed 1994, 141)

Similarly, Stephen Carter has praised religion's potential role as social critic and as a source of governmental *de*-legitimation (or at least, as an institution placing limits on the extent of government authority):

> Religions are in effect independent centers of power, with bona fide claims on the allegiance of their members, claims that exist alongside, are not identical to, and will sometimes trump the claims to obedience that the state makes. A religion speaks to its members in a voice different from that of the state, and when the voice moves the faithful to action, a religion may act as a counterweight to the authority of the state.

. . . For a religion, in its corporate self, will often thumb its nose at what the rest of society believes is right. Democracy needs its nose-thumbers, and to speak of religions as intermediaries is to insist that they play important roles in the proper function of the Republic. (Carter 1993, 35)

It is difficult to overstate the contrast between the passages cited above and the arguments advanced by Reichley and Neuhaus earlier in this chapter. Political religion in the 1980s was valued as a majoritarian, democratic source of government and social authority. The shared nature of American religious and moral commitments was thought to make democratic deliberation and enforcement possible by limiting the range of policy options government might consider. In contrast, political religion in the 1990s is defended as radical, critical, and libertarian, and provides *alternatives* to the authority of public officials. Carter's emphasis on religion as a source of "nose-thumbing" is explicitly antimajoritarian and suggests an enduring tension between the requisites of citizenship and discipleship.

Conclusion

Chapters 3 and 4, taken together, highlight an interesting paradox in the conduct of church-state relations in the contemporary United States. In Chapter 3, it was shown that the Supreme Court, which is the ultimate arbiter of constitutional issues, has taken a much more communalist position on issues of religious free exercise than on other matters. The *Smith* and *Boerne* decisions have indicated quite clearly that the Court cannot be expected to defer to Free Exercise claims in the immediate future, and that the practical scope of the Free Exercise Clause has been limited substantially in the 1990s. Conversely, the public, rhetorical side of the church-state debate has come to value the Free Exercise Clause almost exclusively, at the very point in time at which Free Exercise claims are being viewed most skeptically by the Courts. The resolution (or continuation) of this apparent tension is the subject of the next and final chapter.

Questions for Discussion

1. To what extent does democratic self-governance depend on the existence of generally shared values? If common values are important, how can contemporary political causes such as "multiculturalism" be justified?

2. Is there a moral or religious consensus on fundamental values in the United States? If so, are these primarily religious values, or publicly shared premises derived from a source

other than religion (if the latter, what might this source be)? If not, does this pose a problem for American democracy in the twenty-first century?

3. Does the right of religious free exercise provide a warrant to alter the practices of governmental institutions such as public schools? For example, is the teaching of evolution a violation of the religious liberty of citizens who hold to a literal interpretation of the Bible? Is "scientific creationism" a politically *or* scientifically acceptable means of protecting religious freedom?

4. Is the Christian Right's apparent shift toward a rhetoric of individual rights more consistent with your understanding of the principles underlying democratic politics than the group's previous emphasis on shared religious values? Might such a shift involve an unacceptable compromise of religious values for believers?

5. Is the Religious Liberty Protection Act a "Trojan horse" that could allow religious people to limit the civil liberties of members of other (perhaps unpopular) groups?

Notes

1. All this means is that prior experience is likely to have *some* effect on the formation of character. The question of how much influence an environment exerts is beyond the scope of this study, and is unimportant in the present context.

2. The American value of individualism may to some extent account for the importance of the abortion issue in religious politics in the United States. Abortion clearly involves questions of personal morality; but it also involves the rights of incipient "persons." Unlike homosexuality or adultery, abortion can be described as a crime in which "others" (fetuses) are physically harmed.

3. For a "pro-choice" argument on the abortion issue involving the Establishment Clause, see Wenz (1992).

4. Some analysts have suggested that religion may undermine support for other publicly accessible warrants, such as certain constitutional protections and freedoms. For an overview, see Segers and Jelen (1998).

5. The *Scopes* trial was dramatized, with a good deal of literary license, in the play *Inherit the Wind* (see Wills [1990]).

5

The Future of the Church-State Debate

Proponents of tuition vouchers hope the vouchers will make it easier for parents to send their children to nonpublic schools. Most private schools, such as the Catholic girls' school pictured here, have a particular religious orientation. (Photo © Philip Gould/CORBIS)

In many ways, the late 1990s were difficult years for religious conservatives in the United States. Both long-term and short-term political events provided no evidence of anything approaching a "moral majority" among Americans. Claims that the people adhered to a consensus on the fundamentals of a Judeo-Christian tradition seemed increasingly implausible as the millennium came to an end, and as publicly contested moral issues failed to mobilize mass followings in the United States. A sign in a Clinton campaign office during the 1992 presidential contest read, in part, "It's the economy, stupid." Political events toward the end of the twentieth century appeared to bear out that statement, as concerns for economic growth and justice superseded (though perhaps only temporarily) questions of personal morality.

In late 1998, President Bill Clinton was impeached by the House of Representatives for perjury and obstruction of justice. Clinton's alleged misdeeds were centered around an "inappropriate" sexual relationship between him and a 21-year-old White House intern named Monica Lewinsky. On a close, party line vote, Clinton was impeached on two counts by the House. He was narrowly acquitted of the charges in a Senate trial in early 1999. Aside from the intense partisan divisions evident in the impeachment vote in the two houses of Congress (a theme to which I will return later in this chapter), what stands out about the impeachment controversy was the unresponsiveness of public opinion to the charges of sexual and legal impropriety leveled against President Clinton. Throughout a process that included public charges and countercharges, criminal and civil trials, Clinton's carefully worded (and later discredited) denials of having had "sexual relations with that woman," and the first impeachment of an elected president, Clinton's approval ratings in virtually all public opinion polls stubbornly remained in the range of 60 percent. Despite a year-long scandal, approximately two Americans in three believed Clinton was doing a "good job" as president. Indeed, at the height of the Lewinsky scandal, the Democrats made impressive gains in the off-year elections of 1998. The mid-term elections in Clinton's second term marked the first occasion since 1934 in which the president's party gained seats in the House of Representatives in a mid-term election. Whether Clinton's persistent popularity resulted from public support for a strong economy or from a general respect for the president's privacy, the failure of the

American people to condemn Clinton's apparent moral shortcomings was quite sobering to a number of leaders of the Religious Right. Given clear evidence of serious moral failings on the part of the president, the American people responded with a collective shrug.

In the somewhat longer term, the end of the Clinton administration also marked an important shift in the public debate concerning abortion. Long a central concern of religious conservatives, legalized abortion became an important electoral issue in the 1990s (Abramowitz 1995; Cook, Jelen, and Wilcox 1992, 1994a, 1994b; Adams 1997). Perhaps in response to the Supreme Court's 1989 ruling in *Webster v. Missouri Reproductive Services,* citizens on both sides of the abortion issue began to evaluate candidate and party positions on abortion in making electoral choices at several levels of government. Moreover, the electoral politicization of the abortion issue has revealed the unpopularity of the "pro-life" position. Whatever the morally "correct" position on abortion may be, there exists a growing understanding that supporting a woman's right to terminate a pregnancy intentionally is the politically popular position in the United States today. This in turn has resulted in a strategic shift among many Republican candidates away from strident advocacy of the pro-life position and toward a more nuanced, moderated stance (Neal and von Drehle 1999). As evidenced by Bob Dole's attempt to distance himself from the GOP's antiabortion platform plank in the 1996 election, Republican leaders of all stripes have come to realize how divisive and costly the abortion issue can be. Thus, even among activists for whom abortion is a central political issue, there has been a tendency to concentrate on peripheral aspects of the controversy, such as the legality of so-called "partial birth" (third trimester) abortions, or parental rights in situations in which the availability of abortions to minors is in question (Gray 1999).

These changes may represent the culmination of a trend identified in the preceding chapter: It seems increasingly implausible to assert that in the United States a majority generally supports traditionalist, conservative positions on issues of personal morality. Although Americans may disapprove of adultery, homosexuality, or drug use, there is an increasing reluctance to enforce these values by invoking the power of government. To this extent, it has become problematic for contemporary religious conservatives to argue in favor of an accommodationist reading of the Establishment Clause, because it is by no means clear that a majority of the American people will in fact accommodate either orthodox Christianity or traditional morality. Majoritarian arguments about the "elitist" nature of moral permissiveness are difficult to maintain in light of recent trends in public opinion, and the facile compatibility of Christianity and democracy appears more and more problematic.

The response of Christian Right leaders to current trends has been mixed and confused. Several prominent leaders have suggested that the failure of the Senate to convict Clinton in the 1999 impeachment trial indicates that politics is a futile avenue by which to attempt to advance religious values. Moreover, even religious leaders who seek to remain part of the political process have tended to regroup and adjust their goals for the long term. For example, Pat Robertson, a former U.S. presidential candidate and the founder of Christian Coalition, has suggested that although no "moral majority" exists in the United States, there is a strategically situated moral minority that can alter election outcomes in "swing" states (see *Las Vegas Review-Journal* 1999b).

As noted in Chapter 4, these changes have occasioned a rhetorical shift among religious conservatives from a focus on narrowing the scope of the Establishment Clause to a renewed emphasis on the importance of religious free exercise. This change in focus has been accompanied by an altered understanding of the public role of religion: Rather than a (or *the*) source of moral consensus, religion is viewed as an important, prophetic source of social and political criticism. That is, rather than representing the *actual* preferences of the American population (which have been shown to be inconsistent with the values of doctrinally conservative Christianity), the Christian Right has taken on the task of protecting authentic Christians (a beleaguered minority) from the political and moral threats posed by the larger, secular culture. Moreover, protecting the rights of believing Christians may ultimately provide a platform from which the values that Americans *should* hold can be advanced in the public dialogue.

The Contest over Religious Free Exercise

As noted in Chapter 4, the renewed emphasis on the Free Exercise Clause among religious conservatives is more consistent with the widely held American value of individualism. As adherents of the Christian Right and other religiously motivated activists offer libertarian justifications for their political positions, they seem likely to gain the sympathy, or at least the tolerance, of citizens at other points on the political spectrum. For example, in the case of *Boerne v. Flores* (described in Chapter 3), the American Civil Liberties Union submitted an *amicus curiae* brief on behalf of the archdiocese of San Antonio. The importance of this position on the part of the ACLU is difficult to overstate. An organization with a long tradition of religious separatism effectively switched positions when the issue was cast in terms of religious liberty rather than the public enforcement of religious values.

Ironically, the reassertion of the value of religious free exercise in public discourse has been accompanied by increasing skepticism about Free Exercise claims on the part of the Supreme Court. According to most analysts, the Court drastically narrowed the scope of the Free Exercise Clause in *Employment Division v. Smith*, and reaffirmed that narrow interpretation in *Boerne*. In the process of striking down the Religious Freedom Restoration Act, the Court made the *right* to the free exercise of religion contingent on acts of Congress or of state and local legislatures.

It seems unlikely that the Court will modify or overturn the precedents set in *Smith* and *Boerne* in the foreseeable future. In particular, the Court's ruling in *Boerne* makes clear that the Court's position on the Free Exercise Clause is consistent and thorough. Recall that, unlike the *Smith* case, *Boerne* does not deal with the assertion of religious rights on the part of unpopular or strange religious minorities. The fact that the Court was willing to apply the *Smith* precedent to a "mainstream" (Roman Catholic) parish, which had the unexceptionable goal of expanding seating capacity in its sanctuary, indicates that the scope of *Smith* is not limited to Moonies making pests of themselves at airports, or Santerians engaging in rituals involving animal sacrifice. In the course of the public aspects of worship and ministry, many, if not most, denominations appear likely to have some contact with government. In *Smith* and *Boerne*, the Court has made it clear that religious denominations can expect no extraconstitutional consideration in the pubic sphere. Thus, it might be argued that the Court has created a constitutional doctrine, which can perhaps be termed the *Smith-Boerne* rule: The Free Exercise Clause *only* requires that government refrain from specifically and intentionally discriminating against religious citizens and organizations. The clause does not provide protection for religious practices that violate otherwise valid, neutral laws, absent an explicit legislative exemption.

Moreover, the politics of Supreme Court jurisprudence makes modification of the *Smith-Boerne* precedents unlikely. It is particularly noteworthy that the thrust of the Court's opinion in *Boerne* was devoted to clarification of the Court's powers relative to Congress, to interpret the Constitution, and more specifically to define the scope of Congress's enforcement power under the Fourteenth Amendment. Although the Court held that the incorporation of the Bill of Rights under the Fourteenth Amendment (see Chapter 2) provides federal jurisdiction over local zoning issues such as those raised in *Boerne*, and although it conceded that the Fourteenth Amendment grants Congress the power to enforce the amendment "through appropriate legislation," the Court ruled that the enforcement provision was remedial rather than proactive. That is, Congress could correct egregious violations of the Due Process Clause (such as cases of racial discrimination) under its enforcement power, but it could not affirm new understandings of constitutional preroga-tives. In other words, the Court, and not Congress, has the last word concerning the meaning of any provision in the Bill of Rights. Since *Boerne* not only raises the question of the meaning of the Free Exercise Clause but also calls into question the powers of the federal courts under the separation of powers, it seems unlikely that the Court will acquiesce to a reduction of its power relative to that of Congress. The Religious Freedom Restoration Act posed the Court with a challenge to its au-thority as arbiter of the Constitution, to which the Court responded strongly. As noted in Chapter 3, Congress is attempting to revive this issue, using the Com-merce Clause as the constitutional justification for asserting legislative jurisdiction. At the moment of this writing, it was not clear how the Court would respond to the latest congressional attempt to broaden the scope of the Free Exercise Clause.

The *Smith-Boerne* understanding of the Free Exercise Clause may actually in-crease the coherence of the Court's First Amendment jurisprudence, by making the Court's understanding of religious free exercise more consistent with its read-ing of the Establishment Clause under *Lemon v. Kurtzman*. In terms of the four-fold typology described in the first chapter of this volume, the Court may have moved from the position of religious free-marketeer to that of religious minimal-ist. In his concurring opinion in *Boerne*, Justice Stevens explicitly invoked the Es-tablishment Clause, reaching the same conclusion as the Court's majority. In a manner consistent with the "religious effects" prong of the *Lemon* test (govern-ment may not do anything that has the effect of advancing or inhibiting religion), Stevens argued that application of RFRA to St. Peter's parish in Boerne, Texas, would involve granting an advantage (in this case, an exemption from a local zon-ing regulation) to a religious body—an advantage that would not be available to a secular plaintiff. This religiously preferential policy, argued Stevens, constituted a violation of the Establishment Clause.

Read together, the interpretations of the First Amendment found in *Lemon*, *Smith*, and *Boerne* suggest the emergence of a jurisprudence of religious rights that entails a minimal presence for religion in the public sphere. To overstate for the sake of clarity, the operative precedents in *Lemon* and *Smith* imply that gov-ernment may not help religion except in fairly narrowly drawn circumstances, and government need not afford religion special constitutional protection. The most extreme formulation of contemporary church-state jurisprudence would suggest that government may not provide either general or specific assistance to religion and need not take special care, while passing neutral laws, not to limit the exercise of religious freedom.

Future changes in the Court's composition also seem unlikely to occasion a modification of the *Smith-Boerne* rule. All three dissenters in *Smith* (Harry Blackmun, William Brennan, and Thurgood Marshall) had retired by the time the *Boerne* case was decided. Of the six justices in the *Boerne* majority, only two (William Rehnquist and John Stevens) seem likely as of this writing to retire from the Court in the near future. Among the dissenters in *Boerne* (Sandra Day O'Connor, Steven Breyer, and David Souter), only O'Connor seemed likely in late 1999 to retire soon. As the author of the Court's majority opinion in *Kiryas Joel*, Justice Souter may be amenable to a *Lemon*-based challenge to assertions of Free Exercise, as suggested by Stevens in his *Boerne* concurrence. Thus, regardless of the outcomes of the presidential elections of 2000 and 2004, and the subsequent judicial appointments in the next decade, it seems improbable that changes in the membership of the Supreme Court will result in reconsideration of the *Smith-Boerne* rule.

The Debate Continues

Given the Court's skepticism of Free Exercise claims, and the continuation of the Court's separatist reading of the Establishment Clause in *Everson* and *Lemon*, is there any reason to believe that the issue of church-state relations may eventually be settled? The answer to this question appears to be "no," due in large part to the decentralized nature of political authority. In a parliamentary system, in which relatively disciplined political parties seek to gain power by winning *national* elections, a divisive issue such as the role of religion in public life might well have been disposed of by party elites (see Tatalovich 1995; Lijphart 1975). However, the fragmented nature of political power in the United States places a premium on the formation of *local* majorities. The resulting decentralization of parties and government seems likely to result in the continuation of the church-state debate.

The federal system in the United States, combined with the separation of governmental powers at virtually all levels, ensures that a variety of elective offices will be available to potential candidates. Moreover, the highly decentralized nature of political parties in the United States means that candidates for most offices are self-recruited and can attempt to gain a party's nomination for office (generally, through primary elections) regardless of their positions on particular issues. As noted in Chapter 3, candidates or officials who represent constituencies containing pockets of support for particular (or more general) forms of religious accommodation may have incentives to raise issues involving church-state relations, regardless of the probability that such proposals will actually be enacted.

For example, Christian Scientists adhere to a belief system that encourages them to eschew conventional forms of medical care, such as drugs, surgery, and "standard" techniques of medical diagnosis (e.g., checks for blood pressure and fever). Nevertheless, Christian Science nursing facilities do exist in which patients are kept clean and comfortable and receive the benefit of prayers offered by Christian Science "practitioners." Until quite recently, these nursing facilities had received government funding in the form of Medicare payments. A 1996 lawsuit challenged such funding, with the plaintiff (an organization called Children's Health Care Is a Legal Duty, or CHILD) arguing that government assistance to these facilities entailed an unconstitutional establishment of religion. In response to a judge's ruling overturning the practice of providing Medicare to Christian Science nursing facilities, Senators Edward Kennedy, a liberal Democrat from Massachusetts, and Orrin Hatch, a conservative Republican from Utah, restored a modified version of the payments in an amendment to the Balanced Budget Act of 1997. Another lawsuit from CHILD has been dismissed and is awaiting appeal at this writing (Goldstein 1999). Senator Kennedy has filed an *amicus curiae* brief in which he argues that the payments are necessary in order to preserve the religious freedom of Christian Scientists.

This example illustrates the continuing life of issues involving church-state relations. Senators Kennedy and Hatch both have had a long-standing interest in issues of religious freedom, and both were cosponsors of the Religious Freedom Restoration Act. Moreover, both men were representing key constituencies in this action. Hatch represents the state of Utah, in which a large portion of the population belongs to the church of Latter-Day Saints, often termed Mormons. The LDS has a long history of discrimination for its unconventional beliefs, and Senator Hatch has long supported a strong libertarian view of the Free Exercise Clause. Senator Kennedy, a Roman Catholic, represents a state that contains the largest concentration of Christian Scientists in the nation; and apart from a personal commitment to the protection of religious freedom, his act can be regarded as effectively protecting the religious interests of the people he represents in Congress.

From these examples we may safely conclude that the essentially parochial nature of representation in American politics guarantees that there will always be politicians who are willing to raise issues of church-state relations in public debate. Since elected officials ranging from local school boards to the U.S. Congress represent particular jurisdictions (e.g., townships, legislative districts, and states), circumstances probably will arise in which it will be politically advantageous for some candidates to promote "religious freedom," or the accommodation of religious belief in the public sphere. These advantages may exist regardless of whether the proposed legislation actually is enacted, or once enacted, passes constitutional review by the court system. Where issues involving religious freedom are concerned, it may advantage candidates to have "fought the good fight," regardless of the outcome of religiously based political conflicts.

Furthermore, recent trends in American political life suggest that candidates for elective office will raise religiously charged issues even more often in the immediate future. One important development in the United States during the past generation or so is the increasing independence of the electorate. That is, fewer and fewer citizens identify with a political party, and as a consequence, an increasing number have low levels of political interest and activity (Asher 1992). For a variety of reasons, citizens of the United States do not express support for either the Democrats or the Republicans, nor do they vote with the same regularity as did previous generations.

One prominent exception to the general trend of political dealignment in the American electorate has been the shift toward the Republican party among white evangelical Christians (Kellstedt et al. 1994; Wald 1997). Prior to the 1972 election, many doctrinally conservative Christians who lived in the South traditionally had supported the Democratic party. Others, for primarily theological reasons, had evinced an "otherworldly" orientation and consciously avoided political involvement altogether (Wilcox 1989; Jelen 1987). Due in large part to the identification of the Democratic party with permissive positions on such lifestyle issues as abortion, gay rights, feminism, and drug use, many conservative evangelicals established psychological ties with the GOP. Indeed, in the presidential elections of 1992 and 1996, white evangelicals proved the most loyal supporters of losing Republican candidates George Bush and Bob Dole, despite the slender "evangelical" religious credentials of both men. At the level of the mass public, doctrinally conservative Christians are an important component of any likely winning Republican coalition. It is also important to note that the electoral importance of these religious Republicans is likely enhanced by the relatively low turnout that characterizes most elections in the United States.

The American political process has been penetrated by religion also at the level of political leadership. The Christian Right is a dominant force in several state Republican parties and is a serious competitor for authority within the party in many other states (Rozell and Wilcox 1997). Delegates to national party conventions have increasingly been defined by their religious characteristics, with doctrinally and socially conservative Christians providing an expanding percentage of the Republican party's activist base (Layman 1999). What this means is that Republican *leaders* are more likely to make explicitly religious appeals than they have in past elections, and that an important segment of Republican *voters* seems ready to respond to such public stances. Although it is important to avoid overstatement—religious conservatives have not usually been able to elect very conservative candidates, and conservative positions on some lifestyle issues can be politically costly—it seems clear that the ranks of religious conservatives cannot be ignored in the calculations of any prospective Republican candidate.

A somewhat paradoxical consequence of dealignment within the American electorate has been a partisan polarization among members of legislative bodies in the United States. Most legislative elections, whether at the national, state, or local level, are contested in single-member districts. That is, a given jurisdiction, such as a state or municipality, is divided into districts, each of which typically elects one member to the legislative body in question. Following the national census taken each decade, legislatures in each state capitol redraw maps of electoral districts for elections to the state legislature and to the U.S. House of Representatives. Only the most naive observer of American politics would overlook the possibility that the process of legislative redistricting might be affected by partisan self-interest. Clearly, members of state legislatures seek to redraw district lines so as to maximize the possibilities that certain candidates (or more often, the candidates of certain parties) will be elected. This practice, known as *gerrymandering*, is limited to some extent by the federal courts. Nevertheless, it cannot be denied that even within the limits posed by the judiciary, legislative bodies have a good deal of discretion in the delineation of electoral districts.

What is of particular interest here is the idea that the strategy underlying partisan legislative redistricting appears to have changed, based on the partisan characteristics of the electorate. A standard view of legislative gerrymandering is that a party empowered to draw a legislative map will attempt to isolate supporters of the opposition party into a few very homogeneous districts. This tactic is thought to have the effect of creating a few very safe districts for the opposition, while distributing supporters of the majority party in a number of districts, which in turn makes the majority party competitive in as many districts as possible. For example, if it is assumed that most African Americans are likely to vote for Democratic candidates for Congress and for state legislatures, it is often in the interests of the Republican party to create legislative districts containing large majorities of African Americans rather than to distribute potential Democratic voters across a number of districts in which Republican candidates might be competitive. By conceding a few very safe districts to the Democrats, a Republican majority in a state legislature might maximize its electoral prospects in a number of the remaining districts.

However, Michael McDonald (1998) has suggested that the dominant redistricting strategy might change as the electorate becomes less partisan and more independent. As the psychological ties between voters and political parties weaken, the aggregate behavior of the electorate becomes less predictable. The creation of competitive but relatively safe districts becomes difficult because there are few politically reliable blocs of voters. Under such circumstances, a political party may well seek to reduce its electoral risks by protecting its base, and might attempt to create a few highly safe districts upon which the party can rely.[1] Thus, under the scenario described in the preceding paragraph, the creation of a few highly homogeneous African American districts might become a desirable *Democratic* strategy if it is assumed that there is no reliably Democratic bloc of white voters on which the party can depend. In order to ensure at least a minimal level of representation during periods in which the electorate is highly independent and a party or its candidates are unpopular, legislative party leaders may seek the creation of a secure base of legislative seats. The first order of business in the process of legislative redistricting may be the preservation of a reliable base for the party.

If this argument adequately describes the behavior of contemporary state legislatures, and if it remains the case that white evangelical Christians constitute a highly reliable bloc of Republican voters, we might expect that Republican-controlled legislatures will create districts for U.S. House and state legislative elections that contain very high concentrations of religious conservatives. The representatives of such districts will have strong incentives to raise issues of religious freedom, and to press the limits of the Establishment Clause in creating specific policies. Recall from Chapter 3 that many Americans are abstract separatists but favor state accommodation of religion in specific instances. The general characteristics of public opinion in the United States, in addition to some likely consequences of the politics of legislative districting, suggest that certain members of the U.S. House of Representatives and certain members of state legislatures will have strong electoral incentives to keep issues of church-state relations on the political agenda.[2] Furthermore, if it is assumed that seniority remains at least an informal source of political influence in legislative bodies, then candidates from religiously homogeneous districts may come to wield political power disproportionate to their actual numbers. In certain legislative bodies, such as the U.S. Congress and state legislatures, longevity and experience are important sources of political influence. Over time, one might expect to see religious conservatives attain positions of legislative leadership within the Republican party at an increasing rate.

The current Speaker of the U.S. House of Representatives (Dennis Hastert of Illinois) is an excellent example of this possible trend. Hastert, a graduate of Wheaton College, represents a district in suburban Chicago. Wheaton College is widely known as a prestigious evangelical institution of higher learning,[3] and Hastert's academic credentials are an important signal to religious conservatives that their values and interests will continue to be taken seriously by the Republican party in the House.

The realignment of evangelical Protestants in the face of the general dealignment of the electorate poses a different set of problems for candidates for executive offices (president or governor) or for the U.S. Senate. Since the jurisdictions in which candidates for these offices seek election are typically fixed (state legislatures cannot unilaterally alter a state's boundaries), there is no reason to suppose that persons seeking these types of offices will have incentives to place religious issues on the public agenda. However, the connection between religious conservatives and the Republican party is likely to pose strategic dilemmas for candidates for statewide or national office. During the past generation, it has become increasingly common for party candidates to be nominated through primary elections. In many instances, primaries are characterized by relatively low levels of voter turnout, in which highly motivated and interested citizens constitute a disproportionate share of the primary electorate. If we assume that in some Republican primaries such mobilized voters are likely to be religious conservatives (a reasonable assumption), then it follows that candidates seeking Republican nominations for governor, senator, or president may need to be acceptable to the Religious Right during the primary phase of the electoral cycle, and to take positions favorable to an accommodationist reading of the Establishment Clause or consistent with the symbol of religious freedom. However, in a general election, those same positions may become political liabilities among a more diverse, secular electorate. On the Republican side of the aisle, the strategies necessary to achieve nomination to higher office may conflict with the tactics required to be elected to that office. As veteran political observer and perennial Republican candidate Richard Nixon once observed: "Republicans have to run to the right in the primary, and then to the center in the general election. Of course, this is much easier if the primary is held in Tahiti" (Ambrose 1991). In general elections, the growing class of candidates for legislative office, for executive office, or for the U.S. Senate may have strong disincentives to raise religious issues in their public utterances.[4]

What all this suggests, of course, is that future church-state issues seem increasingly likely to be placed on the political agenda by members of the legislative branch of government. Given the power of the symbol of religious liberty and the growing importance of evangelical Protestants in the Republican party, one would not expect Republican senators, governors, and presidents to overtly resist conservative positions on religious issues. However, the major impetus for placing such issues on the political agenda may well lie in Congress and in state legislatures across the country. I cautiously predict that in the first decade of the twenty-first century, the separation of powers between legislative and executive branches of government will become an increasingly hostile division on religious issues, and that this tension will occur regardless of the partisan coloration of either branch.

The combination of a religiously assertive legislature with a passive but compliant executive will have important implications for the litigation of claims of religious liberty. Given that the Supreme Court seems unlikely to modify the *Smith-Boerne* rule in the foreseeable future, plaintiffs who press Free Exercise claims in the courts are unlikely to succeed. There are two possible (and nonexclusive) legislative reactions to this situation: First, Congress or state legislatures could continue to pass versions of the Religious Freedom Restoration Act, in the hope of finding a formulation that the Supreme Court would approve. Even if such measures were to be defeated in Congress or struck down by the judiciary, individual legislators might derive electoral benefits from introducing such legislation. It thus seems likely that the Court will have several more opportunities to reaffirm (or if I am mistaken, to modify or reverse) the *Smith-Boerne* rule.

Second, legislative bodies may provide precise, religiously based exemptions from general laws in a manner specifically contemplated in Scalia's majority opinion in *Smith*. A legislature might well exempt religious organizations from local zoning ordinances, antidiscrimination laws, or other government policies that seem to restrict religious liberty. Under such circumstances, dissenters from this sort of religiously based exemption might well engage in litigation under the Establishment Clause. As Justice Stevens argued in his concurrence in *Boerne,* if the acts of a legislature provide advantages to religious organizations that are not available to their secular counterparts, such policies may well violate the Court's interpretation of the Establishment Clause in *Lemon*. If the ability to discriminate in hiring or in the provision of services has value (which it may in some circumstances), such exemptions may violate the Establishment Clause by providing advantages for members of the religious groups who are relieved of the burden of compliance with certain civil rights statutes (see Choper 1995).

The Changing Scope of Religious Free Exercise

If the foregoing analysis is correct, it seems likely that the Free Exercise Clause will become (or has already become) the main focus of political conflict for contemporary issues of church-state relations. It remains to be considered whether the Free Exercise Clause will bear the weight placed on it by religiously motivated political activists in the twenty-first century. To what extent can issues of interest to religious conservatives be subsumed under the rubric of religious free exercise?

If recent analysts of the proper relationship between religious bodies and government are correct, the Free Exercise Clause may be quite adaptable to a variety of political issues. In Chapter 4, we saw that it is possible to describe perennial issues such as school prayer and the teaching of evolution as questions of religious free exercise. Similar accounts of other issues of interest to religious conservatives also seem amenable to recasting in a Free Exercise light.

A number of states and localities have passed measures prohibiting discrimination against homosexuals in employment, housing, or the granting of credit. However, religious opponents to such measures have argued that the right of religious free exercise includes the right to choose one's social and business associates on the basis of shared beliefs and lifestyle practices, and to shun those whose behavior is proscribed by one's religious principles. Can a Christian landlord legally be required to provide shelter for gay couples (or for that matter, for heterosexual couples who are cohabiting outside of marriage), who are practicing a lifestyle that the Bible describes as an "abomination"? Could it not be argued on the basis of Scripture that a landlord who provides shelter to such individuals is sinning in the eyes of the Lord?

This example is not merely hypothetical. As I wrote this chapter, in 1999, the Nevada state legislature had just passed a measure prohibiting discrimination against gays in the area of employment. The passage of this bill evoked a strong reaction from a lobbyist for the conservative Eagle Forum: "It [the bill] creates a situation in Nevada where employers' rights of freedom of religion and speech and association are undermined. . . . We already have under the Constitution equal rights for everyone. Now we have special rights for homosexuals" (Vogel 1999).

Note the advantage of characterizing antidiscrimination measures as a violation of the Free Exercise Clause. Religious activists morally opposed to homosexuality need not persuade citizens of other moral perspectives that homosexuality is somehow "objectively" immoral. Such persuasion has proven quite difficult, since some Americans apparently have few reservations about the propriety of homosexual behavior, and many more regard sexual acts between consenting adults as matters best assigned to a private sphere of activity. Even some people who regard sexual relations between members of the same sex as sinful are not necessarily willing to impose legal or public penalties on such acts. All that is required under a Free Exercise rationale for opposition to antidiscrimination policies is that adherents of certain religious traditions sincerely *believe* homosexuality to be immoral, and that the Constitution requires that public policies defer to such religious beliefs.

Such arguments seem unlikely to prevail in courts under the *Smith-Boerne* rule. However, given the political opportunities that moral/religious issues offer to certain members of Congress or candidates for state and local legislative office, it is not difficult to imagine that some representatives will seek religion-based exemptions from antidiscrimination measures. Within very broad limits, legislators may and often do create exceptions to the laws they pass, and the symbolic popularity of the idea of religious liberty may make such exemptions increasingly attractive.

Perhaps more generally, religious conservatives have long invoked the notion of "family values" as a rhetorical means by which the application of individual liberty may be limited. That is, since the notion that "consenting adults" should be granted a great deal of latitude in their private behavior is widely accepted in contemporary American discourse, citizens who hold traditionalist positions on lifestyle issues often invoke the effects of such behaviors on children as reasons for restricting the behaviors. Children often are not considered capable of meaningful consent, and their involuntary exposure to morally questionable communications and practices may be considered harmful—especially insofar as they are incapable of evaluating such behaviors (see Jelen 1999).

A very controversial issue in the late twentieth century was the possible government regulation of pornographic material transmitted over the Internet. The Internet is a highly decentralized, computer-based means of electronic communication, to which both producers and consumers of information have very easy access. A substantial amount of information available over the Internet is of a sexually explicit nature, including high-definition photographs and illustrations. Because it has proven difficult to restrict the access of minors to this sort of material, Congress has passed several measures that would restrict access to this material by Internet users (for example, by requiring that a valid credit card number be provided before access to a sexually oriented Website would be granted).[5] Thus far, these measures have been struck down by the courts as unconstitutional infringements on freedom of expression. This result is understandable, since the issue posed has balanced a legislative act intended to produce a socially desirable outcome against a fundamental, constitutionally protected right. The courts have traditionally been very reluctant to approve limits on freedom of speech or the press, and restrictions on free expression have typically been drawn quite narrowly.

However, it might be possible to support restrictions on Internet access to sexually explicit material on Free Exercise grounds. Although no one to my knowledge has attempted such an argument, it might be argued that government support for unlimited access to the Internet (via support for the physical infrastructure of the Net, or via *.edu* accounts, available to participants in educational institutions without charge) may violate the Free Exercise Clause. If one assumes (plausibly, in my view) that the right of religious free exercise minimally includes the right to raise one's children in one's own religious faith, one easily could argue that government-sponsored programs that undermine this form of religious freedom are at least constitutionally suspect. Although under *Smith-Boerne* it seems unlikely that a religiously conservative parent would have cause for legal action against a provider of electronic "smut," the possibility of religiously motivated legislative exceptions is specifically contemplated (and approved) in Scalia's majority opinion in *Smith*.

The probable judicial reaction to such a strategy is far from clear. Instead of pitting a legislatively mandated outcome (no dirty pictures for children) against a constitutional right (free expression), describing the limitation of Internet access to sexually explicit material as a protection of religious freedom would pit two First Amendment rights (free expression and religious free exercise) against one another. In American jurisprudence, constitutional rights generally trump legislative mandates; but conflict between different (and perhaps opposing) constitutional rights is a different matter altogether. It is unclear whether the right of a provider of electronic pornography to distribute sexually explicit material necessarily supersedes the right of parents to protect their children from such communications in the course of the children's upbringing. It is also unclear, under *Smith-Boerne*, whether Congress must defer to the rights of the Internet provider in such instances of potentially conflicting constitutional rights.

In contrast, it is clear that the issue of tuition tax vouchers will be an important area of church-state conflict in the immediate future. As noted in the first chapter of this book, tuition tax vouchers allow the parents of children enrolled in private schools the opportunity to count the tuition they have paid to such institutions either as a tax deduction (which would involve subtracting the amount of tuition from the parents' taxable income) or as a tax credit (which would permit parents to deduct the cost of tuition directly from their tax bill). Parents whose income falls below the threshold necessary to take advantage of such tax benefits receive direct payments or tax vouchers to offset the cost of private education.

The secular argument for such vouchers is quite appealing: As the people with primary responsibility for the education of their children, parents should have the right to choose among different educational institutions. Imposing "additional" costs on parents via public school taxes is thought to inhibit (practically, if not legally) parental choice. Given the fact that everyone must pay taxes, vouchers may be regarded as a simple means of restoring a parental prerogative that existed prior to the advent of public education. It also has been suggested that absent some sort of tax break for the parents of private school students, public schools enjoy a quasimonopoly in primary and secondary education, which reduces the incentives of public schools to provide high-quality education for their students.

If attendance at alternative private schools were more readily available (i.e., less costly), the competition between educational institutions might encourage schools of all types to be more effective and less costly.

Of course, there are numerous potential problems with most voucher proposals. Some of the more practical questions include whether private institutions would be subject to state accreditation standards; whether private schools could simply raise tuition to match the cost of the vouchers; and whether most parents have the pedagogical sophistication to choose intelligently among competing educational institutions.[6] However, for present purposes, the most important issue raised by the possibility of tuition vouchers is a constitutional one: Since most observers agree that a large majority of private institutions are affiliated with religious denominations, would not such indirect financial assistance to church-related schools constitute a proscribed establishment of religion? Indeed, since the most extensive network of parochial schools in the United States is operated by the Roman Catholic church, might not tuition vouchers violate even an accommodationist understanding of the Establishment Clause by providing practical, preferential benefits to Catholicism?

Here again, it is possible to describe the various voucher proposals in a manner consistent with the Free Exercise Clause. If the right of religious free exercise guarantees that parents may educate their children in the faith of their choice, then does not the "double taxation" imposed by state-supported public education not infringe on the rights of the parents (and their children) to exercise their religious beliefs? Arguably, if the exercise of a fundamental constitutional right (in this instance, religious free exercise) is rendered costly by government policies, has not the right been unconstitutionally limited?

The issue of tuition tax vouchers, then, starkly evokes the tension between the Establishment and Free Exercise clauses described at the beginning of this book. Moreover, a legal contest over this issue may be unusually attractive for those who seek government accommodation of the public exercise of religious belief. Aside from the obvious rhetorical appeal of the symbols of "freedom," "school choice," and so on, vouchers might under some interpretations pass the *Lemon* test and thus avoid the issue of religious establishment. Recall that the three-part test in *Lemon v. Kurtzman* proscribes policies that have the intent of advancing or inhibiting religion or the effect of advantaging or disadvantaging religion, or that result in "excessive entanglement" between government and religious bodies. It seems reasonably clear and straightforward to suggest that tuition tax vouchers pass the first and third parts of the *Lemon* test rather easily. Given public dissatisfaction with the state of contemporary public education, the idea of increasing the range of educational opportunities available to students seems, on its face, to be a valid secular purpose. Indeed, some proponents of vouchers have argued that such tax benefits or income transfers would be of primary benefit to students who are members of minority groups in large, urban areas, whose schools are often of very low quality. Arguably, the provision of vouchers may have some of the characteristics of a civil rights policy. For example, a voucher plan recently passed in Florida would restrict eligibility for vouchers to the parents of students whose public schools failed to meet state-mandated minimum academic requirements (Holmes 1999). Moreover, the fact that vouchers are directly provided to families rather than to schools suggests that the problems of "entanglement" between church and state could also be minimal. If the point of tuition vouchers is to provide choices of educational institutions, there is no reason to suppose that the choice of a religious institution would require any particular government supervision of the use of tax benefits.[7]

It seems at least possible, then, that the Establishment Clause issues raised by tuition vouchers could be confined to the second prong of the *Lemon* test: Does the payment of vouchers produce an effect favorable to the advancement of religion? The *Lemon* test prohibits inadvertent, as well as intentional, government promotion of religion. The resolution of this question might ultimately depend on a factual claim: Would most students taking advantage of a voucher program attend religious schools? And if so, would the aggregation of such individual choices represent a constitutional violation? Opponents of tuition vouchers could easily demonstrate that most vouchers would be used to cover the costs of religious education, which would create a presumption against the constitutionality of vouchers. Opponents could counter this argument in one of two ways. First, it might be argued that the choices of parents do not constitute government policy per se, and that it is not the responsibility of government to guarantee or prohibit certain outcomes in a market-based competition. In other words, if most recipients of vouchers independently elected to use the money to attend religious schools, so what? Arguably, it is stretching a point to accuse government of proscribed religious establishment if government simply provides neutrally defined assistance of which religious bodies take greatest advantage.

Second, proponents of vouchers have suggested that more private schools (which might or might not be religious in nature) might be started up, once tuition vouchers became generally available. That is, the existence of a voucher program might provide private educators with incentives to offer primary and secondary education on a "for-profit" basis, if the government (through the tax code) made such profits more likely. The possibility that vouchers might result in the greater availability of private, secular education could indicate that the connection between vouchers and religious education is either the result of neutral market forces or a historical accident. In either case, such a pattern of individual choices perhaps should not be the basis for rejecting a popular, apparently reasonable policy on constitutional grounds.

As discussed in Chapter 3, the Supreme Court recently approved limitations and qualifications to the *Lemon* test. Opinions rendered in the 1993 case of *Zobrest v. Catalina Foothills School District* and in the 1997 case of *Agostini v. Felton* suggest that the Rehnquist Court is willing to modify the *Lemon* test as applied to parochial schools. A case involving the constitutionality of school vouchers might provide a vehicle for the Court's fundamental reconsideration of the *Lemon* test. Although precedents are very important in the Supreme Court's decisionmaking processes, they are not absolute, and they have occasionally been reversed. Historically, precedents have been limited and qualified by a string of decisions before being formally overturned (see Richard Kluger's *Simple Justice* [1977] for a detailed account of this process in cases of racial discrimination). The current signs indicate that the issue of tuition tax vouchers will provide an opportunity for the Court to reconsider its separatist ruling in *Lemon*. Indeed, as I wrote this chapter in 1999, the U.S. Supreme Court had just heard oral arguments for a case *(Mitchell v. Helms)* concerning the narrow question of whether public money can be used for computer equipment and other instructional materials for parochial schools. This case (which has been joined by the Clinton administration) may provide an opportunity for the Court to reconsider its generally separatist ruling in *Lemon* (Greenhouse 1999).

One reason why judicial review of school voucher programs seems likely is that such programs are politically quite popular and thus may provide opportunities for elected officials to enhance their political fortunes. School vouchers may indeed create a common ground between two "wings" or factions of the Republican party: the social conservatives, who are primarily concerned with issues of personal morality; and the libertarian conservatives, whose highest priority is reducing government interference in the private sector of the economy. Political candidates seeking the support of both wings of the party might emphasize the opportunities vouchers offer for religious education among groups of religious conservatives, focusing on the tax-reduction features of a system of tuition tax credits among Republicans for whom economic issues are more salient. Whereas some issues (e.g., abortion) tend to expose the tension between these two ideological groups in the Republican party, the voucher issue seems to tap concerns common to each. Moreover, this issue appears to exacerbate certain tensions within traditionally Democratic constituencies—for example, among African Americans. In Florida, for example, the National Association for the Advancement of Colored People (NAACP) has endorsed a system of vouchers, whereas the Urban

League of Greater Miami has expressed opposition to vouchers. In general, it appears that poorer African Americans, whose children are likely to attend low-quality public schools (and who may be relatively more religious), are generally supportive of vouchers, whereas more affluent blacks are somewhat more skeptical (Holmes 1999).

Thus, it can be anticipated that Republican candidates for a variety of offices will keep the issue alive in the foreseeable future. Indeed, as of this writing, the state of Florida has passed a rather generous voucher program at the initiative of Governor "Jeb" Bush. Similar programs are under consideration in a number of states, and pose complex questions of religious establishment and free exercise. At this writing, courts in Wisconsin and Ohio have ruled that vouchers do not violate the Establishment Clause, but a Maine court has found vouchers unconstitutional on grounds of religious establishment. Minnesota and Arizona provide tax credits both to recipients of tuition vouchers and to contributors to private charities that provide school vouchers, respectively (Janofsky 1999). Among other states, Illinois has recently passed a tax credit version of a voucher bill, which is awaiting a court test at this writing (Kloehn 1999).

Some Normative Considerations

There are practical reasons for suggesting that the question of church-state relations is unlikely ever to be resolved in a neat, intellectually coherent fashion. Even if such a resolution were possible, would it be desirable? It is my contention that it would not.

My view that a continuation of the church-state debate is desirable is based on three general observations about religious politics in the United States. Firstly, *the practical meaning of the Establishment Clause must become broader as the population becomes more religiously diverse.* Despite the eloquence and venom of Scalia's dissent in *Kiryas Joel,* the notion of religious establishment can no longer be confined to formal, legal, state establishments of a single religion. The possibility of a positive manifestation of governmental "neutrality" toward religion becomes ever more elusive as fewer and fewer Americans adhere to even a broadly construed Judeo-Christian tradition. Although the U.S. population is generally more religious than those of other Western industrial nations, intense religious belief and frequent religious observance are by no means universal. A large and politically significant minority of Americans do not identify with any religious tradition in any but the most nominal sense, and can be considered secular for most practical purposes (see Kellstedt and Green 1993). Moreover, such secular individuals are represented disproportionately in highly visible institutions such as universities and the news and entertainment media.

Furthermore, a growing number of Americans are affiliating with unconventional, "New Age" religions, or are asserting an individual spirituality while rejecting institutional religion. In *Habits of the Heart* (1985), Robert Bellah and his collaborators described the beliefs of a young woman named Shelia Larson, who called her belief system "Sheliaism." This creed did not involve affiliation with any organized religious denomination but simply consisted of adherence to her "own small voice." It is difficult to imagine a set of "positively neutral" policies that would benefit the increasing numbers of "Shelias" in the United States. In addition, the most recent waves of immigration to the United States (a nation that defines itself in large part as a haven for persecuted immigrants) consist largely of non-Europeans who do not in any fashion adhere to a Western religious tradition. As discussed in Chapter 3, there are definite limits to the willingness of many Americans to provide neutral support to all religions, when "all religions" includes traditions that lie outside the Judeo-Christian worldview ("I don't want my children praying to Buddha"). It is difficult to imagine how government could provide general assistance to all religions in such a religiously diverse nation, while remaining compliant with the Constitution and the Bill of Rights. Even if one were to concede that positive neutrality was possible at the nation's founding, that historical moment has long passed.

A second principle underlying my view of the necessity of the ongoing church-state debate is that *religious freedom must apply to the public sphere* (Witte 1999). That is, it is unreasonable to assert that the right of religious free exercise is protected, if citizens cannot act upon their religious beliefs in public arenas such as politics. Religious freedom cannot be maintained if people are not permitted to apply their most cherished and deeply held beliefs to influence government. This observation suggests that a constitutional order in which religious liberty is valued will of necessity deal with the claims and preferences of religiously motivated citizens. Because not all Americans share such motivation, the limits of both the Establishment and the Free Exercise clauses will continually be tested by self-governing citizens seeking to translate their preferences into public policies.

Thirdly, *religious free exercise often requires government support* (Witte 1999). Although the ideas of personal independence and individual sovereignty resonate positively with the current American political culture, the notion that groups or individuals can get along "on their own" is increasingly implausible. It is a commonplace that modern society is characterized by a high level of interdependence, within which individuals pursue their own interests and values. The tuition voucher example presented earlier in this chapter summarizes the resulting dilemma. Since education has become an important *public* function, the concept of neutrality is elusive with respect to religious schools. Imposing the burdens of citizenship (in this case, taxation) without providing corresponding benefits can quite plausibly be characterized as a denial of religious liberty.

If these three principles are well founded, then the issue of church-state relations cannot be resolved in a satisfactory manner—that is, one that serves the requisites both of citizenship and of discipleship. This point can be further illustrated by reference to the four approaches to church-state politics outlined in the first chapter. Two in particular—Christian preferentialism and religious minimalism—seem possible candidates for stable resolutions of the tension between the Establishment and Free Exercise clauses but are arguably unacceptable on normative grounds, as outlined below. The other two models—religious free market and religious nonpreferentialism—are perhaps normatively more attractive, but given certain plausible empirical claims, are likely to be transformed into different styles of religious politics.

Christian preferentialism (the accommodationist-communalist tendency) might indeed be consistent with a simple understanding of democratic politics. If the majority is indeed Christian, why should the majority be prevented from enacting public policies based on its values? The answer, of course, is that preferentialism for the majority creed would constitute a clear violation of the Establishment Clause. Moreover, it seems likely that the Free Exercise rights of religious minorities would receive scant protection in a majoritarian system. It is clearly inconsistent with the value of religious liberty to make one's religious freedom contingent on the content of one's beliefs. A system based on Christian preferentialism would thus do serious damage to the notion that religious liberty is a constitutionally guaranteed *right*, which lies (or should lie) beyond the reach of a popular majority (see Davis 1996).

Similarly, religious minimalism (the separatist-communalist tendency) is a model of church-state relations on which I have commented favorably elsewhere (Segers and Jelen 1998). The problem with a minimalist public role for religion is that it imposes a substantial burden on those whose religious beliefs require them to act in ways that are unpopular, or in extreme cases, illegal. The idea that religious liberty can be confined to a private sphere of activity *that government defines* makes the notion of a *right* to religious freedom available only to the most inoffensive creeds imaginable. What happens to members of locally unpopular religions under policies dominated by religious minimalism? This is not just a question of the rights of a few, isolated abortion providers, Satanists, or Native Americans. As a former Roman Catholic, I have encountered negative reactions to the fact that my faith seemed to require allegiance to a foreign head of state (the pope) or the fact that the rituals of my faith were (until the mid-1960s) conducted in a foreign tongue (Latin). During certain periods of American history (as recently as the 1960 election), it may have been imprudent for Catholics to submit to a popular vote on their religious liberty, since in the minds of many Americans this religious affiliation evoked questions of national loyalty and national identity (Prendergast 1999). Thus, even if government does not provide overt assistance to religion (in a manner consistent with *Lemon*), it is easy to imagine that apparently neutral government policies could infringe on the religious liberty of many Americans. Although adherents to certain creeds might admire or venerate martyrs, a nation that would require the martyrdom or religious abnegation of entire classes of people cannot be said to value religious free exercise (Davis 1996). Of course, martyrdom has not traditionally been associated with social or political life in the United States. Legal penalties for the exercise of religious belief are uncommon in the United States precisely because Americans have traditionally accorded great deference to citizens' assertions of religious liberty. Were minimalism to become the dominant interpretive framework for church-state relations, stark choices between the obligations of citizenship and those of discipleship would likely become much more common.

In contrast to these two fairly unattractive models of church-state relations, religious nonpreferentialism (the accommodationist-libertarian tendency) might seem relatively appealing. What would be the problem if government were to support all religions neutrally and allow for a wide range of religious freedom? The answer to this question appears to be that nonpreferentialism is fairly unstable and could easily be transformed in the United States into a version of Christian preferentialism. The reason for this can be found in the discussion of public opinion in Chapter 3. Recall that many Americans are abstract libertarians but concrete communalists. That is, it is quite common for American citizens to express strong support for the idea of religious liberty but to favor restrictions on practical applications of religious free exercise when presented with the religious practices of strange or unpopular groups. The sociological study mentioned in Chapter 3 (Jelen and Wilcox 1995) makes clear that many Americans are uncomfortable with the idea of genuine religious diversity. If the free exercise of religion entails the right to attempt to translate one's preferences into government policy, then the majority might well restrict the religious liberty of members of faiths whose practices seem harmful or strange to them.

Alternatively, a nonpreferentialist politics might involve scrupulous protection for the religious liberty of members of marginalized faiths. That is, a libertarian understanding of the Free Exercise Clause would usually involve placing most aspects of religious freedom beyond the reach of a popular majority. There are at least two potential problems with this approach. Firstly, a strong libertarian commitment to religious liberty would most likely enhance the lawmaking power of the courts as protectors of freedom of religion. As noted in Chapter 2, this might well exacerbate an already undemocratic feature of American politics. Secondly, and more seriously, the granting of religion-based exemptions from otherwise valid laws (as in *Sherbert-Yoder*) might well violate the Establishment Clause. If such exemptions are in fact generally valuable, is not government establishing a preference for one faith over another by granting this sort of exception?

For example, if *Employment Division v. Smith* had been decided differently, and Native Americans had been granted (or had retained) the right to use peyote in their religious rituals, it might be argued that the Court had permitted discrimination in favor of the religious plaintiffs. If indeed the right to ingest hallucinogenic drugs has value (an assertion I certainly would have made as an undergraduate), then one could plausibly argue that the government has discriminated in favor of a Native American religion (and against Catholicism or Methodism) by granting such a dispensation (see Choper 1995). Moreover, if the state government of Oregon (in the case of *Smith*) had sought to permit the ritual use of peyote as a narrowly drawn exception to a general prohibition against such drugs, then it might well be required to monitor the legal use of peyote. Such government monitoring could well violate the "excessive entanglement" prong of the *Lemon* test.

Lastly, the religious free-market approach to church-state relations (the separatist-libertarian tendency) seems likely, over time, to convert to religious minimalism. This prediction is based on the third principle discussed above, which states that on some occasions, the protection of religious liberty requires government support. If government ostensibly permits a wide range of religious practices (by refraining from imposing explicit limitations) but denies religious organizations benefits available to secular bodies, the exercise of religious freedom may eventually become the exclusive prerogative of the affluent. For example, the denial of government support for Christian Science health-care facilities (which eschew "standard" medical services such as drugs and surgery) might well impede the Free Exercise rights of Christian Scientists by making their exercise of religious liberty costly. More generally, the requirement of "no government support" would almost certainly have the effect of handicapping religions whose adherents do not have extensive private means. The rights of religious free exercise might be extended to all citizens, but some citizens might be "more equal" than others. In sum, it is difficult to imagine a resolution of the issues involved in church-state relations that does justice to both the Establishment and the Free Exercise clauses (Davis 1996).

Stephen V. Monsma and J. Christopher Soper (1997), in comparing church-state relations in the United States with those in Australia, the Netherlands, Germany, and England, found the United States less effective at preserving religious freedom than these other Western nations precisely because of the uniquely American provision of "no religious establishment." Monsma and Soper argue that the protection of religious liberty in the United States could be enhanced by limiting the scope of the Establishment Clause and emphasizing the rights of religious free exercise. I disagree. Like Derek Davis (1996) and Clarke Cochran (1990), I suggest that the tension between the requirements of the Establishment and the Free Exercise clauses is in fact healthy both for democracy and for religion in the United States. The fact that the U.S. government must confront the values of a religious citizenry serves as a constant reminder that a system of *self*-government must attend to values that transcend the mere act of governing. Politics is often characterized as "the art of the possible." However, it is quite easy for those most thoroughly engaged in political life (activists, candidates, and others) to lose sight of the idea that democratic politics should exist in the service of some set of (perhaps inconsistent) higher ideals, and that politics is not, for most citizens, an end unto itself. Conversely, the requirement that religious citizens either participate in the public life of the nation or risk being consumed by it arguably has a positive effect on religion as well. Although many definitions of religion emphasize its "otherworldly" character (Choper 1995), the requirements of democratic citizenship remind religious leaders and citizens alike that an authentic faith has consequences for the manner in which believers live. As anyone who has engaged in political life knows, involvement in the public sphere is often a rather humbling experience. Among believers, such humility is often valued, but it also can be elusive within the community of belief. The involvement of religious believers in politics serves to remind citizens of the higher aspirations toward which religious faith points. Likewise, politics can serve to remind believers of the limitations within which discipleship can and must operate.

Conclusion

This discussion has now come full circle. I began this volume with an exploration of American exceptionalism. I argued that the uniquely American interactions between religion and politics have two principal sources. First, the decentralized nature of American government provides incentives for various political leaders to raise issues of faith and politics persistently. Both federalism and the separation of powers place a premium on the formation of local majorities, some of which may value the injection of religious values into political discourse. Second, the coexistence of the Establishment and the Free Exercise clauses as the "First Free-doms" guaranteed by the Bill of Rights suggests a continuing tension between freedom *from* religion and freedom *of* religion. The task of government in such a regime entails protecting the state from unbridled religious activity, protecting the rights of believers from the government, and protecting religious (and irreli-gious) citizens from one another.

The question of church-state relations has a continuing life in American poli-tics and is unlikely to be resolved in the immediate future in any final fashion. The apparently simple task of "render[ing] unto Caesar that which is Caesar's, and render[ing] unto God that which is God's" is complicated by the fact that many issues fall under the jurisdictions of both the sacred and the secular. It is thus dif-ficult to imagine how issues of religious freedom and church-state separation can ever be resolved under our current constitutional format. I would have it no other way. We are, as Justice William O. Douglas asserted, "a religious people," with a natural desire to see our most sacred beliefs and values enacted in public policy. We are also a people that values personal and spiritual autonomy as well as free-dom from government interference. These distinct yet complementary aspects of our national character will continue to fuel conflicts over church-state relations for a long time to come.

Questions for Discussion

1. Is conflict over the appropriate political role of religion inevitable in American poli-tics, or can the issue of church-state relations ever be resolved? Does the frequent appear-ance of church-state issues on the political agenda enhance or detract from democratic politics in the United States?

2. How do other nations deal with questions of religious freedom? Is the United States superior to other nations in this regard, or can we profit from other nations by example? Which nations?

3. Recall the comments of the attorney quoted in Chapter 1, who expressed concern about the "Devil's religion." Do the religion clauses of the First Amendment require us to be neutral about the *content* of different religions? If so, is such a requirement reasonable, or would it make sense to argue that some religions are, in fact, better than others?

Notes

1. In the language of game theory, such a tactic is termed a "mini-max" strategy, in which an actor seeks to minimize the probability that the worst possible outcome (in this case, winning no seats in a legislative election) will occur.

2. Although the Clinton-Lewinsky scandal was not specifically a church-state issue, McDonald's account may explain why the House of Representatives insisted on impeaching President Clinton, despite numerous public opinion surveys suggesting that such an action would be generally unpopular. If we assume that some legislative districts have been drawn to maximize partisan (Republican) homogeneity, and that House members respond to public opinion in their home districts rather than to the nationwide distribution of political attitudes, then the apparently counterintuitive action of the House becomes more easily understandable.

3. Lyman A. Kellstedt, who is a member of the Wheaton faculty, has referred to Wheaton as the "Vatican of Evangelicalism."

4. A belief in a highly conservative GOP primary electorate is quite widespread, but it is not clear whether such a belief is founded in reality. A body of research (Norrander 1989; Cook, Jelen, and Wilcox 1992) has suggested that primary electorates generally are not ideologically more extreme or more consistent than the population as a whole, nor are Republican primary electorates more distinctively "pro-life." However, the most important consideration may be the extent to which candidates *believe* they must "run to the right" in GOP primaries.

5. Internet providers of sexually oriented material have objected to this provision on the grounds that potential consumers often wish to view samples of the material before incurring costs or revealing their identities to Website proprietors.

6. This last argument is particularly compelling to some providers of public education (including me). Some analysts have suggested that the application of economic terminology (*competition, monopoly,* and so on) to education is misguided. In most areas, consumers are the ultimate arbiters of the "quality" of products or services. However, most of us would insist that there are external criteria by which educational quality can be evaluated. In particular, the business adage that "the customer is always right" seems inappropriate when applied to schools (parents and children presumably being the "customers") (see Wrinkle et al. 1999; Smith and Meier 1995).

7. This issue becomes somewhat more complicated if the question of state accreditation of private institutions is raised. If states were to require schools at which vouchers could be redeemed to meet state-mandated academic and/or political standards (e.g., no state aid to institutions that practice racial discrimination), then the imposition of accreditation by a public body might raise the Free Exercise question (i.e., Does state regulation of a religious institution's curriculum constitute a limitation of religious free exercise?).

Appendix
Selected Supreme Court Decisions

Marbury v. Madison, 5 U.S. (1 Cranch) 137 (1803). Dismissed Marbury's petition for a writ of mandamus to gain federal office. Established a precedent for the Court's power of judicial review.

Slaughterhouse Cases, 83 U.S. (16 Wall) 36 (1872). Limited the scope of the Privileges and Immunities Clause of the Fourteenth Amendment. Made Due Process and Equal Protection clauses principal vehicles for protecting civil liberties from infringement by state governments.

Reynolds v. United States, 98 U.S. 145 (1879). Upheld federal criminal law prohibiting polygamy and denied a Mormon's free exercise claim to the practice. Distinguished between beliefs (which could not be regulated) and actions (which could).

Chicago, Burlington, and Quincy Railroad Co. v. Chicago, 166 U.S. 225 (1897). The first case in which a liberty listed in the Bill of Rights was "incorporated" to include protection from infringement by a state government.

Weeks v. United States, 232 U.S. 383 (1914). Established "exclusionary rule" (disallowing presentation of illegally obtained evidence in criminal trials) for criminal cases in federal courts.

Cantwell v. Connecticut, 310 U.S. 296 (1940). Free Exercise Clause expressly applied to the states through the Fourteenth Amendment; overturned a city licensing law requiring religious groups to obtain licenses before engaging in solicitation.

Minersville School District v. Gobitis, 310 U.S. 586 (1940). Public school requirement of saluting and pledging allegiance to the American flag does not merit Free Exercise exemption.

West Virginia State Board of Education v. Barnette, 319 U.S. 157 (1943). Overruled *Gobitis;* First Amendment provides exemption from mandatory participation in rituals that parties conscientiously oppose—including saluting the flag in a public school classroom.

Everson v. Board of Education, 330 U.S. 1 (1947). Applied the Establishment Clause to the states through the Fourteenth Amendment, but upheld the practice of states' providing school bus transportation to religious and public school children alike.

Zorach v. Clauson, 343 U.S. 306 (1952). Upheld the constitutionality of granting students released time from public schools to attend religious education or services; such released time does not violate Establishment Clause.

Brown v. Board of Education of Topeka, 347 U.S. 483 (1954). Ruled segregation of public schools by race a violation of the Equal Protection Clause of the Fourteenth Amendment. This case is widely regarded as an instance of judicial activism by the Warren Court.

Mapp v. Ohio, 367 U.S. 643 (1961). Incorporates exclusionary rule established in *Weeks* as applicable to states under the Due Process Clause of the Fourteenth Amendment.

Engel v. Vitale, 370 U.S. 421 (1962). Disallowed state program of daily (nondenominational) prayer in public school classrooms, as a violation of the Establishment Clause.

Abingdon Township School District v. Schempp, 374 U.S. 203 (1963). Mandatory Bible reading in public school classrooms held to violate the Establishment Clause.

Sherbert v. Verner, 374 U.S. 398 (1963). Free Exercise Clause forbids state to deny unemployment compensation to claimant discharged from a job requiring work on the Sabbath.

Chamberlain v. Public Instruction Board, 377 U.S. 402 (1964). Reading of Bible and recitation of Lord's Prayer in public school is unconstitutional establishment of religion.

United States v. Seeger, 380 U.S. 163 (1965). Persons claiming exemption from military service for religious reasons may qualify for conscientious objector status if their belief is "sincere and meaningful" and occupies in their life "a place parallel to that filled by the God of those admittedly qualifying for the exemption." Requires broad interpretation of Selective Service Act.

Griswold v. Connecticut, 381 U.S. 479 (1965). Strikes down Connecticut anticontraception statute; locates constitutional right of privacy in penumbra of Third, Fourth, and Fifth Amendments.

Loving v. Virginia, 388 U.S. 1 (1967). Extended *Griswold* precedent to invalidate a Virginia statute prohibiting interracial marriage.

Epperson v. Arkansas, 393 U.S. 97 (1968). Ruled that a state criminal law prohibiting the teaching of evolution in a public school or state university entails an unconstitutional establishment of religion.

Walz v. Tax Commission, 397 U.S. 664 (1970). Upheld state property tax exemption for church property against Disestablishment Clause challenge.

Welsh v. United States, 398 U.S. 333 (1970). Persons whose consciences, "spurred by deeply held moral, ethical, or religious beliefs," do not allow them to be an "instrument of war" are entitled to conscientious objector status, regardless of whether such beliefs are "religious" in the narrow sense.

Lemon v. Kurtzman, 403 U.S. 602 (1971). Establishment Clause requires laws to have (1) a secular purpose and (2) a secular effect (a primary effect that neither advances nor inhibits religion); and (3) not to entail "excessive entanglement" between church and state.

Wisconsin v. Yoder, 406 U.S. 205 (1972). Based on the Free Exercise Clause, exempted Amish children from compulsory public school attendance.

Eisenstadt v. Baird, 405 U.S. 438 (1972). Extended right of privacy to unmarried couples seeking to obtain contraceptive devices.

Norwood v. Harrison, 413 U.S. 455 (1973). State may loan textbooks on secular subjects to religious schools, but not if those schools discriminate on racial grounds.

Levitt v. Committee for Public Education and Religious Liberty, 413 U.S. 472 (1973). States may not reimburse religious schools for most costs incurred to administer standardized tests and to prepare mandated state records.

Roe v. Wade, 410 U.S. 113 (1973). Established limited constitutional right to abortion under privacy right articulated in *Griswold.*

Meek v. Pittenger, 421 U.S. 349 (1975). State may loan textbooks to religious schools, but not other supplies or personnel, even if those were mandated by state policy.

Wolman v. Walter, 433 U.S. 229 (1977). State may provide various personnel, diagnostic services, and standardized testing to religious schools, but may not lend instructional materials to private schools or to parents or provide transportation for field trips organized by religious schools.

Stone v. Graham, 449 U.S. 39 (1980). Struck down a state statute that required the posting of the Ten Commandments on the wall of each public school classroom.

Bob Jones University v. United States, 461 U.S. 574 (1983). Upheld an IRS decision to revoke federal tax exemption from a religious university that engaged in religiously based racial discrimination.

Marsh v. Chambers, 463 U.S. 783 (1983). Upheld state practice of appointing legislative chaplains to offer prayers at the General Assembly against a challenge based on the Establishment Clause.

Lynch v. Donnelly, 465 U.S. 668 (1984). Upheld government practice of displaying Nativity scene as part of holiday display in city park against charge that such display constituted a state establishment of religion.

Wallace v. Jaffree, 472 U.S. 38 (1985). Struck down state law providing for moments of silence (for prayer or meditation) in public schools as violation of Establishment Clause.

Grand Rapids School District v. Ball, 473 U.S. 373 (1985). States may not lend public school personnel to religious schools to teach remedial and enrichment courses.

Aguilar v. Felton, 473 U.S. 402 (1985). States may not use public school teachers to administer remedial educational programs to indigent children in classrooms leased from religious schools.

Bowers v. Hardwick, 478 U.S. 186 (1986). Upheld a state antisodomy statute against a claim that such a measure violated the right to privacy articulated in *Griswold.*

Edwards v. Aguillard, 482 U.S. 578 (1987). Struck down a state statute that required, in public schools, the teaching of both creation and evolution, if a theory of origins was taught at all, as a violation of the Establishment Clause under *Lemon.*

Michael H. v. Gerald D., 109 S. Ct. 2333 (1989). Upheld a state law denying parental rights to a man claiming to have fathered a child born to a woman married to another man. Occasioned articulation of Scalia's "specificity" standard in constitutional interpretation.

Frazee v. Illinois Department of Employment Security, 489 U.S. 829 (1989). The state may not deny unemployment benefits to a claimant for refusing to take a job that might require working on the Sabbath.

County of Allegheny v. ACLU, 492 U.S. 573 (1989). Disallowed the county's practice of allowing a privately funded Nativity scene in front of the county courthouse, but permitted the inclusion of a menorah in a public display.

Webster v. Reproductive Health Services, 109 S. Ct. 2040 (1989). Limited the right to abortion in *Roe v. Wade* by upholding several state restrictions on the delivery of abortion services.

Employment Division v. Smith, 494 U.S. 872 (1990). Denial of unemployment compensation benefits to Native American who was discharged for sacramental use of peyote, a proscribed narcotic, does not violate Free Exercise Clause. Limited Free Exercise rights articulated in *Sherbert* and *Yoder.*

Lee v. Weisman, 505 U.S. 577 (1991). Ecumenical prayer by a Jewish rabbi at a public school graduation ceremony violates the Establishment Clause.

Lee v. International Society for Krishna Consciousness, 505 U.S. 830 (1992). Ban on distribution of religious materials in airport terminals is invalid under the First Amendment, since the restriction does not satisfy a standard of "reasonableness."

Lamb's Chapel v. Center Moriches Union Free School District, 508 U.S. 384 (1993). Public school that opens its facilities, during nonschool time, to various voluntary community groups must provide equal access; may not exclude only those with religious viewpoint.

Church of the Lukumi Babalu Aye v. City of Hialeah, 508 U.S. 520 (1993). Local ordinance prohibiting ritual sacrifice of animals violates the Free Exercise Clause.

Zobrest v. Catalina Foothills School District, 509 U.S. 1 (1993). The state's provision of an interpreter to a disabled student at a religious high school does not violate the Establishment Clause.

Board of Education of Kiryas Joel Village School District v. Grumet, 512 U.S. 687 (1994). The state's creation of a single public school district within an exclusively Satmar Hasidic community constitutes unlawful establishment of religion.

U.S. v. Lopez, 514 U.S. 549 (1995). Invalidated the congressionally mandated Gun-Free School Zones Act of 1990, rejecting the U.S. assertion of congressional powers as overbroad. The first case in sixty years to limit the authority of the federal government under the Commerce Clause.

Agostini v. Felton, 521 U.S. 203 (1997). Overturned *Aguilar;* the mere presence of a state employee in a religious institution is not per se unconstitutional, and thus the state may provide remedial services to students at religious schools.

City of Boerne v. Flores, 521 U.S. 507 (1997). The Religious Freedom Restoration Act (1993), which required use of the compelling state interest test for Free Exercise cases, was declared unconstitutional, at least as applied to the state. Invalidated Congress's attempt to overturn *Smith* through legislation.

Schundler v. American Civil Liberties Union, 104 3d 1435 (1997). The Court allowed to stand a lower court ruling that banned (on Establishment grounds) a holiday display containing a Nativity scene, a Hanukkah menorah, and a Christmas tree.

Glossary

Accommodationism   A narrow interpretation of the Establishment Clause in which government is forbidden only to provide assistance to particular churches. Accommodationists believe that neutral government support for religion in general is permissible.

American Center for Law and Justice   A conservative religious group, founded by the Rev. Marion "Pat" Robertson, that seeks to protect religious liberty. The ACLJ represents Christians who believe they have been the victims of discrimination.

American Civil Liberties Union   A long-standing interest group in American politics that exists to protect the constitutional rights of American citizens. The ACLU is unpopular among members of the Christian Right.

American exceptionalism   A belief that the United States is a unique nation and thus is not directly comparable with other nations.

Americans United for the Separation of Church and State (AUSCS)   An interest group founded by television producer Norman Lear, which opposes any form of governmental support for religion.

Amicus curiae   Literally, "friend of the court"; an advisory brief submitted to a court by a person or organization not named as a party in the case or controversy being considered by the court.

Bread for the World   An ecumenical religious organization dedicated to fighting world hunger.

Burger Court   The United States Supreme Court during the period in which Warren Burger was chief justice (1969–1986). The Burger Court was generally expected to reverse some of the tendencies of the Warren Court, and move the Court in a more conservative direction. However, in the area of church-state relations, the Burger Court is best known for its ruling in *Lemon v. Kurtzman*, which is generally considered a strongly separationist interpretation of the Establishment Clause.

Catholic Alliance   An organization founded in 1995, which was intended to attract Catholic support for the Christian Right.

Christian Coalition   An interest group founded by the Rev. Marion "Pat" Robertson, which seeks a more assertive role for religion in American public life.

Christian preferentialism   The combination of an accommodationist reading of the Establishment Clause with a communalist reading of the Free Exercise Clause. Communalists believe that nondiscriminatory government assistance to religious bodies is permissible, and that government may generally regulate unorthodox or unpopular religious practices.

Civil religion   The veneration of symbols and artifacts of the American political system or political culture (e.g., the flag and the Constitution).

Communalism   A narrow interpretation of the Free Exercise Clause in which government is forbidden to single out religious practices for specific regulation. Communalists hold that otherwise neutral laws that have the effect of restricting religious practices are constitutionally permissible. Often contrasted with libertarianism.

Concerned Women for America   An evangelical Christian women's group that focuses primarily on family issues.

Court-packing   An attempt by President Franklin D. Roosevelt in 1937 to tilt the balance of the Supreme Court in a more liberal direction by adding new justices to that body if any sitting justice did not retire by the age of 70. The policy was widely unpopular, and it was never approved by Congress.

Due Process Clause   The clause in the Fourteenth Amendment that prohibits state governments from depriving citizens of life, liberty, or property without "due process of law." During the twentieth century, the Due Process Clause provided a constitutional basis for the doctrine of incorporation, which applies certain rights in the Bill of Rights to the actions of state and local governments.

Eagle Forum   An antifeminist organization headed by Phyllis Schlafly. Initially organized in opposition to the Equal Rights Amendment, this group now opposes legal abortion, secular humanism, and feminism.

Establishment Clause   A portion of the First Amendment that limits government assistance or sponsorship of religion: "Congress shall make no law respecting an establishment of religion."

Evangelical Protestantism   A large branch of American Protestantism that is partially defined by a strong view of the authority of the Bible. Evangelicalism includes, but is not limited to, fundamentalism, Pentecostalism, and charismatic Christianity.

Evangelicals for Social Action   A liberal group of evangelical Protestants concerned with issues such as poverty, homelessness, and environmental protection.

Evolving standards   A theory of constitutional interpretation that holds that the provisions of the U.S. Constitution must be read with contemporary standards and values firmly in mind. This position stands in stark contrast to the theory of original intent.

Family Research Council   An organization of the Christian Right, headed by Gary Bauer, which specializes in detailed policy analyses of public issues.

***Federalist* papers**   A series of newspaper editorials written by Alexander Hamilton, James Madison, and John Jay between 1787 and 1789, urging ratification of the U.S. Constitution. The *Federalist* papers are considered by some to be an important source for determining the intentions of the framers of the Constitution.

Free Exercise Clause   The clause in the First Amendment that limits government regulation of religion. "Congress shall make no law . . . prohibiting the free exercise thereof" (of religion).

Free-marketeer, Religious   A person holding a libertarian view of the Free Exercise Clause, and a separationist view of the Establishment Clause. Free-marketeers hold that government is generally forbidden to provide assistance to religion and is subject to very strict limitations in the legal regulation of religious belief and practice.

Great Society   A set of ambitious social programs, generally associated with the administration of Lyndon B. Johnson (1963–1969). The Great Society programs dramatically increased the scope of governmental authority.

Incorporation   The doctrine of constitutional interpretation that holds that the provisions of the Bill of Rights limit the actions of state and local governments as well as those of the federal government. Incorporation is generally justified by reference to the Due Process Clause of the Fourteenth Amendment.

Interpretivism   A theory of constitutional interpretation that requires justices to use only the language contained in the Constitution to ascertain the meaning of any given passage. Interpretivism resembles the theory of original intent (see below) in its emphasis on textual analysis, but does not permit the use of historical documents beyond the Constitution in efforts to arrive at an accurate constitutional understanding.

Judicial activism   A term (usually pejorative) describing the tendency of some justices to institute new, sweeping legal changes through judicial decisions. Often used to describe the Warren Court.

Judicial review   The power of American courts to invalidate acts of legislatures by declaring them unconstitutional, or inconsistent with the Constitution.

JustLife   An organization dedicated to the preservation of human life; opposes war, capital punishment, abortion, and euthanasia.

Libertarianism   In the context of church-state relations, the belief that government may restrict the free exercise of religion only under extremely limited conditions. Contrasted with communalism, libertarianism implies a very broad reading of the Free Exercise Clause.

Minimalist, Religious   A person who adheres to a communalist understanding of the Free Exercise Clause and a separationist interpretation of the Establishment Clause. Religious minimalists hold that government generally may not assist religion in any form but has broad discretion in regulating religious practices.

Moral Majority   One of the earliest and most famous Christian Right organizations, Moral Majority was founded by the Rev. Jerry Falwell in 1979 and was disbanded in 1990.

Multiple establishment   The governmental provision of direct (often financial) support to several religions. Multiple establishment was a common practice in a number of states prior to the adoption of the U.S. Constitution.

New Deal   A set of government programs established by President Franklin D. Roosevelt (1933–1945) to assist economically disadvantaged citizens during the Great Depression. The New Deal substantially altered the nature and scope of government in the United States.

Nonpreferentialism   A belief in an accommodationist reading of the Establishment Clause. Nonpreferentialists believe that neutral, nondiscriminatory government assistance to religious bodies is constitutionally permissible.

Nonpreferentialism, Religious   Combines an accommodationist interpretation of the Establishment Clause with a libertarian view of the Free Exercise Clause. Religious nonpreferentialists believe that government may provide assistance to religion in general and that its authority to regulate religious practice is extremely limited.

Original intent A theory of constitutional interpretation that holds that in order to derive the correct meaning from a constitutional provision, one must ascertain the intentions of the framers. Original intent, or originalism, is often contrasted with judicial activism, or arguments that involve the concept of evolving standards.

Party discipline The ability of party leaders to reward or punish party members (typically, members of a leglislature) for compliance or noncompliance with leadership demands.

Pax Christi A liberal Catholic organization that seeks to "establish peace and justice." Pax Christi is particularly concerned with promoting governmental policies designed to help the poor.

Penumbra The "shadow" of specific rights defined in the Bill of Rights, on the basis of which the existence of other, more general rights has been inferred. In the case of *Griswold v. Connecticut,* Justice William O. Douglas identified a constitutional right to privacy in the penumbra of the Third, Fourth, and Fifth Amendments to the Constitution.

People for the American Way (PAW) An organization founded by television producer Norman Lear, which promotes freedom of expression and a narrow view of the Establishment Clause.

Public accessibility The ethical requirement that justifications for public policy choices in a democracy be offered in terms that are understandable to all citizens.

Rehnquist Court The U.S. Supreme Court during the tenure of William Rehnquist as chief justice (1986–present). The Rehnquist Court is generally considered more conservative than its predecessors, and this Court has limited the scope of the Free Exercise Clause.

Religious Freedom Restoration Act (RFRA) An act of Congress passed in 1993, intended to restore the *Sherbert-Yoder* standard for religious free exercise and to overrule the Supreme Court's decision in *Employment Division v. Smith.* Held unconstitutional by the Supreme Court in *City of Boerne v. Flores.*

Religious Liberty Protection Act (RLPA) A 1999 proposal in Congress that would overrule the Supreme Court's limited interpretation of the Free Exercise Clause in *Smith* and *Boerne.*

Religious Right A series of social movements intended to reverse a perceived trend toward secularism and moral relativism. Organizations such as Eagle Forum, Family Research Council, Moral Majority, and Christian Coalition are considered to occupy the Religious Right (also known as the *Christian Right*).

Rights Individual prerogatives that are often considered "natural" and that are held by individuals regardless of government policies. Typically, rights can be properly limited by governments only for very strong, compelling reasons.

Rutherford Institute A conservative, international legal organization dedicated to the protection of civil rights. The Rutherford Institute provided legal support for Paula Jones in her sexual harassment suit against President Bill Clinton.

Scientific creationism A doctrine founded on the belief that a literal interpretation of the account of the creation of the world in the Book of Genesis is verifiable through contemporary methods of scientific inquiry. Often contrasted with "evolutionism" or "Darwinism."

Self-determination The ethical right of citizens in democratic systems to make choices affecting the formation of their own preferences and characters, and to undertake actions in keeping with those choices.

Separation of powers The feature of the U.S. Constitution that provides for three independent branches of government at the federal level: legislative, executive, and judicial.

Separatism The doctrine that government should maintain neutrality between religion and secularism, based on a belief that the Establishment Clause prohibits all government involvement with religion.

Strict constructionism A school of constitutional interpretation that holds that constitutional provisions should be read as narrowly as possible.

Tenth Amendment A provision in the Bill of Rights that explicitly limits the jurisdiction of the federal government: "The powers not delegated to the United States by the Constitution, nor prohibited by it to the states, are reserved to the States respectively, or to the people." Applications of the Tenth Amendment have been limited by the doctrine of incorporation.

Warren Court The U.S. Supreme Court during the term of Chief Justice Earl Warren (1953–1969). The Warren Court is widely regarded as having engaged in a considerable amount of judicial activism: It limited public assistance to parochial schools, held that organized prayer in public schools was unconstitutional, and advanced a strongly libertarian interpretation of the Free Exercise Clause.

References

Abramowitz, Alan I. 1995. "It's Abortion, Stupid: Policy Voting in the 1992 Presidential Election." *Journal of Politics* 57: 176–186.

Adams, Greg D. 1997. "Abortion: Evidence of Issue Evolution." *American Journal of Political Science* 41: 718–737.

Ambrose, Stephen. 1991. *Nixon: Ruin and Renewal, 1973–1990.* New York: Simon and Schuster.

American Civil Liberties Union (ACLU). 1994. "RLPA Reconsidered." Available on line at www.aclu.org/congress/1012599a.html (cited January 25).

Americans United for the Separation of Church and State (AUSCS). 1999. "School Prayer Measure Reintroduced." Available on line at www.au.org (cited October 15).

Anastopolo, George. 1981. "The Religion Clauses of the First Amendment." *Memphis State University Law Review* 11 (Winter): 189–190.

Asher, Herbert. 1992. *Presidential Elections in American Politics: Candidates and Campaigns Since 1952.* 5th ed. Pacific Grove, Calif.: Brooks-Cole.

Audi, Robert. 1989. "Separation of Church and State and the Obligations of Citizenship." *Philosophy and Public Affairs* 18: 258–296.

Bellah, Robert N., Richard Madsen, William M. Sullivan, Ann Swidler, and Steven M. Tipton. 1985. *Habits of the Heart: Individualism and Commitment in American Life.* Berkeley: University of California Press.

Berger, Peter. 1967. *The Sacred Canopy: Elements of a Sociological Theory of Religion.* New York: Doubleday.

Berman, Marshall. 1970. *The Politics of Authenticity.* New York: Atheneum.

Biskupic, Joan. 1994. "Special School District Ruled Unconstitutional." *Washington Post,* June 28: A1, A10.

Blanchard, Dallas A. 1994. *The Anti-Abortion Movement and the Rise of the Religious Right: From Polite to Fiery Protest.* New York: Twayne.

Blanchard, Dallas A., and Terry J. Prewitt. 1993. *Religious Violence and Abortion: The Gideon Project.* Gainesville: University of Florida Press.

Bork, Robert H. 1990. *The Tempting of America: The Political Seduction of the Law.* New York: Free Press.

Boston, Rob. 1997. "Making Amends." *Church and State* 50 (May): 4–8.

Bradley, Gerard V. 1987. *Church-State Relationships in America.* Westport, Conn.: Praeger.

Bragg, Rick. 1998. "Vision of Community Guided by Hand of God." *New York Times,* December 30: A10.

Brisbin, Richard A. 1992. "The Rehnquist Court and the Free Exercise of Religion." *Journal of Church and State* 34: 57–76.

Buchanan, James M., and Gordon Tullock. 1962. *The Calculus of Consent.* Ann Arbor: University of Michigan Press.

Buell, Emmett, and Lee Sigelman. 1985. "An Army That Meets Every Sunday? Popular Support for the Moral Majority." *Social Science Quarterly* 66: 426–434.

———. 1987. "A Second Look at 'Popular Support for the Moral Majority: A Second Look.'" *Social Science Quarterly* 68: 167–169.

Burns, Gene. 1992. *The Frontiers of Catholicism: The Politics of Ideology in a Liberal World.* Berkeley: University of California Press.

Burns, James McGregor. 1963. *The Deadlock of Democracy.* Englewood Cliffs, N.J.: Prentice-Hall.

Carmines, Edward G., and James A. Stimson. 1980. "The Two Faces of Issue Voting." *American Political Science Review* 79: 78–91.

Carter, Stephen L. 1993. *The Culture of Disbelief: How American Law and Politics Trivialize Religious Devotion.* New York: BasicBooks.

Casanova, Jose. 1994. *Public Religions in the Modern World.* Chicago: University of Chicago Press.

Chapman, Steve. 1998. "The Gospel According to . . . : New York Schools Create a Religious Martyr." *Chicago Tribune,* July 12: A15. Available on line at www.chicagotribune.com.

Chicago Tribune. 1998. "Jews' Suit Against Yale Is Dismissed." August 8 (Section 1): 8.

Choper, Jesse. 1995. *Securing Religious Liberty.* Chicago: University of Chicago Press.

Christian Coalition. 1998. "House Passes RFA." Available on line at www.cc.org (cited June 10).

Cloud, John. 1999. "Law on Bended Knees." *Time,* September 13: 32–33.

Cochran, Clarke E. 1990. *Religion in Public and Private Life.* New York: Routledge.

Cohen, Adam. 1998. "Victory for Vouchers." *Time,* June 22: 38.

Converse, Phillip E. 1964. "The Nature of Belief Systems in Mass Publics." Pp. 206–261 in *Ideology and Discontent,* ed. David Apter. New York: Free Press.

———. 1966. "Religion and Politics: The 1960 Election." Pp. 96–124 in *Elections and the Political Order,* by Angus Campbell, Phillip E. Converse, Warren E. Miller, and Donald E. Stokes. New York: John Wiley and Sons.

Cook, Elizabeth Adell, Ted G. Jelen, and Clyde Wilcox. 1992. *Between Two Absolutes: Public Opinion and the Politics of Abortion.* Boulder: Westview.

———. 1994a. "Issue Voting in U.S. Senate Elections: The Abortion Issue in 1990." *Congress and the Presidency* 21: 99–112.

———. 1994b. "Issue Voting in Gubernatorial Elections: Abortion and Post-*Webster* Politics." *Journal of Politics* 56: 187–199.

Cord, Robert. 1982. *Separation of Church and State: Historical Fact and Current Fiction.* New York: Lambeth Press.

Curry, Thomas J. 1986. *The First Freedoms: Church and State in America to the Passage of the First Amendment.* New York: Oxford University Press.

Dahl, Robert. 1956. *A Preface to Democratic Theory.* Chicago: University of Chicago Press.

David, Rene, and John E. Brierly. 1978. *Major Legal Systems of the World.* New York: Free Press.

Davis, Derek H. 1996. "Resolving Not to Resolve the Tension Between the Establishment and Free Exercise Clauses." *Journal of Church and State* 38: 245–259.

Driesbach, Daniel L. 1997. "'Sowing Useful Truths and Principles': The Danbury Baptists, Thomas Jefferson, and the 'Wall of Separation.'" *Journal of Church and State* 39: 455–502.

_____. 1999. "Thomas Jefferson and New England Baptists: Reflections on Two Symbols of American Church-State Relations." Paper presented at the annual meeting of the American Political Science Association, September 2–5, Atlanta.

Dugger, Celia W. 1996. "Tug of Taboos: African Genital Rite vs. U.S. Law." *New York Times,* December 28: A1, A8.

Dworkin, Ronald. 1997. "Comment." Pp. 115–128 in *A Matter of Interpretation: Federal Courts and the Law,* by Amy Guttman. Princeton: Princeton University Press.

Elifson, Kirk W., and C. Kirk Hadaway. 1985. "Prayer in Public Schools: When Church and State Collide." *Public Opinion Quarterly* 49: 317–329.

Falwell, Jerry. 1980. *Listen, America!* Garden City, N.Y.: Doubleday.

Fauser, Patricia, Jeanne Lewis, Joel A. Setzen, Finian Taylor, and Ted G. Jelen. 1995. "Conclusion: Perspectives on the Politics of Abortion." Pp. 177–199 in *Perspectives on the Politics of Abortion,* ed. Ted G. Jelen. Westport, Conn.: Praeger.

Finke, Roger, and Rodney Stark. 1992. *The Churching of America, 1776–1990.* New Brunswick, N.J.: Rutgers University Press.

Fleet, Elizabeth, ed. 1946. "Madison's 'Detached Memoranda.'" *William and Mary Quarterly* 3: 535–562.

Formicola, Jo Renee, and Hubert Morken, eds. 1997. *Everson Revisited: Religion, Education, and Law at the Crossroads.* Lanham, Md.: Rowman-Littlefield.

_____. 1999. *The Politics of School Choice.* Lanham, Md.: Rowman-Littlefield.

Fowler, Robert Booth, Allen D. Hertzke, and Laura R. Olson. 1998. *Religion and Politics in America: Faith, Culture, and Strategic Choices.* Boulder: Westview.

_____. 1999. *Religion and Politics in America: Faith, Culture, and Strategic Choices.* Revised ed. Boulder: Westview.

Friendly, Fred W., and Martha J. H. Elliot. 1984. *The Constitution: That Delicate Balance.* New York: Random House.

Glendon, Mary Ann. 1991. *Rights Talk.* New York: Free Press.

Glock, Charles Y., and Rodney Stark. 1968. *American Piety.* Berkeley: University of California Press.

Goddstein, Laurie. 1998. "Town's Logo Becomes a Religious Battleground." *New York Times,* June 23: A1, A17.

Goldstein, Avram. 1999. "It's Faith, but Is It Health Care?" *Washington Post National Weekly Edition,* March 29: 30.

Gray, Jerry. 1999. "A New Political Strategy Is Energizing Opponents of Abortion." *New York Times,* May 24: A27.

Green, John C. 1995. "Pat Robertson and the Latest Crusade: Religious Resources and the 1988 Presidential Campaign." *Social Science Quarterly* 74: 157–168.

Greenawalt, Kent. 1988. *Religious Convictions and Political Choice.* New York: Oxford University Press.

Greenhouse, Linda. 1994. "High Court Bars School District Created to Benefit Hasidic Jews." *New York Times,* June 28: A1, D21–D22.

———. 1999. "Church-State Issue Returns to High Court." *New York Times,* December 2: A25.

Guth, James L., and John C. Green. 1989. "God and the GOP: Religion Among Republican Activists." Pp. 223–242 in *Religion and Political Behavior in the United States,* ed. Ted G. Jelen. New York: Praeger.

Hamilton, Alexander, James Madison, and John Jay. 1937. *The Federalist.* New York: Modern Library.

Hartz, Louis. 1955. *The Liberal Tradition in America.* New York: Harcourt, Brace, and World.

Hertzke, Allen D. 1988. *Representing God in Washington: The Role of Religious Lobbies in the American Polity.* Knoxville: University of Tennessee Press.

———. 1989. "Faith and Access: Religious Constituencies and the Washington Elites." Pp. 259–274 in *Religion and Political Behavior in the United States,* ed. Ted G. Jelen. New York: Praeger.

Hofrenning, Daniel J. B. 1995. *In Washington but Not of It: The Prophetic Politics of Religious Lobbyists.* Philadelphia: Temple University Press.

Holmes, Steven A. 1999. "Black Groups in Florida Split over School Voucher Plan." *New York Times,* May 30: A15.

Hunter, James Davison. 1980. "The New Class and the Young Evangelicals." *Review of Religious Research* 22: 155–169.

———. 1991. *Culture Wars: The Struggle to Define America.* New York: BasicBooks.

———. 1994. *Before the Shooting Begins: Searching for Democracy in America's Culture War.* New York: Free Press.

Iannaccone, Laurence. 1990. "Religious Practice: A Human Capital Approach." *Journal for the Scientific Study of Religion* 29: 297–314.

Janofsky, Michael. 1999. "Ohio Justices Strike Down Voucher Plan in Cleveland." *New York Times,* May 28: A16.

Jelen, Ted G. 1987. "The Effects of Religious Separatism on White Protestants in the 1984 Presidential Election." *Sociological Analysis* 48: 30–45.

———. 1991. *The Political Mobilization of Religious Beliefs.* Westport, Conn.: Praeger.

———. 1993. *The Political World of the Clergy.* Westport, Conn.: Praeger.

———. 1999. "On the Hegemony of Liberal Individualism: A Reply to Williams." *Sociology of Religion* 60: 35–40.

Jelen, Ted G., and Clyde Wilcox. 1990. "Evangelicals and Political Tolerance." *American Politics Quarterly* 18: 25–46.

———. 1995. *Public Attitudes Toward Church and State.* Armonk, N.Y.: M. E. Sharpe.

_____. 1997. "Conscientious Objectors in the Culture War?: A Typology of Church-State Relations." *Sociology of Religion* 58: 277–288.

_____. 1998. "Context and Conscience: The Catholic Church as an Agent of Political Socialization in Western Europe." *Journal for the Scientific Study of Religion* 37: 28–40.

Jelen, Ted G., and Clyde Wilcox, eds. Forthcoming. *The One and the Many: Religion and Politics in Comparative Perspective.* New York: Cambridge University Press.

Johnson, Gerald. 1999. "Montgomery Wars: Religion and Alabama Politics." *Religion in the News* (Spring): 6–8.

Kellstedt, Lyman A., and John C. Green. 1993. "Knowing God's Many People: Denominational Preference and Political Behavior." Pp. 53–71 in *Rediscovering the Religious Factor in American Politics,* eds. David C. Leege and Lyman A. Kellstedt. Armonk, N.Y.: M. E. Sharpe.

Kellstedt, Lyman A., John C. Green, James L. Guth, and Corwin E. Smidt. 1994. "Religious Voting Blocs in the 1992 Election: The Year of the Evangelical?" *Sociology of Religion* 55: 307–326.

Kirk, Russell, ed. 1986. *The Assault on Religion.* New York: University Press of America.

Kloehn, Steve. 1999. "Tax Credit to Test City Catholic Schools as Much as Law." *Chicago Tribune,* June 4: A9. Available on line at www.chicagotribune.com.

Kluger, Richard. 1977. *Simple Justice.* New York: Vintage Books.

Labi, Nadya. 1999. "Holy Owned: Is It Fair for a Catholic Hospital to Impose Its Morals on Patients?" *Time,* November 15: 85.

Labow, Patricia. 1980. *Advanced Questionnaire Design.* Boston: Abt Books.

Las Vegas Review-Journal. 1999a. "Plan for Bible-Based Town Rejected." April 14: 10A.

_____. 1999b. "Robertson Seeks to Reinvigorate Christian Coalition for 2000." October 3: 10A.

Layman, Geoffrey C. 1999. "Culture Wars in the American Party System: Religious and Cultural Change Among Partisan Activists Since 1972." *American Politics Quarterly* 27: 89–121.

Leege, David C. 1993. "Religion and Politics in Theoretical Perspective." Pp. 3–25 in *Rediscovering the Religious Factor in American Politics,* eds. David C. Leege and Lyman A. Kellstedt. Armonk, N.Y.: M.E. Sharpe.

Leege, David C., and Lyman A. Kellstedt. 1993. "Religious Worldviews and Political Philosophies: Capturing Theory in the Grand Manner through Empirical Data." Pp. 216–231 in *Rediscovering the Religious Factor in American Politics,* eds. David C. Leege and Lyman A. Kellstedt. Armonk, N.Y.: M. E. Sharpe.

Levy, Leonard W. 1986. *The Establishment Clause.* New York: Macmillan.

_____. 1988. *Original Intent and the Framers' Constitution.* New York: Macmillan.

Lichter, S. Robert, Stanley Rothman, and Linda S. Lichter. 1986. *The Media Elite.* Bethesda, Md.: Adler and Adler.

Lijphart, Arend. 1975. *The Politics of Accommodation: Pluralism and Democracy in the Netherlands.* 2nd ed., revised. Berkeley: University of California Press.

Lipset, Seymour Martin, and Earl Raab. 1981. "The Election and the Evangelicals." *Commentary* 71: 25–31.

Malbin, Michael. 1978. *Religion and Politics: The Intentions of the Authors of the First Amendment.* Washington, D.C.: AEI Press.

Martin, Alfred R., and Ted G. Jelen. 1989. "Knowledge and Attitudes of Catholic College Students Regarding the Creation-Evolution Controversy." Pp. 83–92 in *Religion and Political Behavior in the United States,* ed. Ted G. Jelen. New York: Praeger.

Maxwell, Carol J. C. 1995. "Introduction: Beyond Polemics and Toward Healing." Pp. 1–20 in *Perspectives on the Politics of Abortion,* ed. Ted G. Jelen. Westport, Conn.: Praeger.

McConnell, Michael. 1998. "Protecting Our Tradition of Religious Liberty." *Chicago Tribune,* July 17 (Section 1): 13.

McDonald, Michael. 1998. "Redistricting, Dealignment, and the Political Homogenization of the House of Representatives." Paper presented at the annual meeting of the American Political Science Association, Boston, September.

McDowell, Gary L. 1993. "The Explosion and Erosion of Rights." Pp. 18–35 in *The Bill of Rights in Modern America,* eds. D. Bodenhammer and J. Ely, Jr. Bloomington: Indiana University Press.

Moen, Matthew. 1989. *The Christian Right in Congress.* Tuscaloosa: University of Alabama Press.

_____. 1990. "Ronald Reagan and the Social Issues: Rhetorical Support for the Christian Right." *Social Science Journal* 27: 119–207.

_____. 1992. *The Transformation of the Christian Right.* Tuscaloosa: University of Alabama Press.

Monsma, Stephen V. 1993. *Positive Neutrality: Letting Religious Freedom Ring.* Westport, Conn.: Praeger.

Monsma, Stephen V., and J. Christopher Soper. 1997. *The Challenge of Pluralism: Church and State in Five Democracies.* Lanham, Md.: Rowman-Littlefield.

Murley, John A. 1988. "School Prayer: Free Exercise of Religion or Establishment of Religion?" Pp. 5–40 in *Social Regulatory Policy: Moral Controversies in American Politics,* eds. Raymond Tatalovich and Byron W. Daynes. Boulder: Westview.

Neal, Terry M., and David von Drehle. 1999. "Abortion Moves Off the GOP Radar Screen." *Washington Post National Weekly Edition,* April 26: 11.

Neuhaus, Richard John. 1984. *The Naked Public Square.* Grand Rapids, Mich.: Eerdmans.

Neustadt, Richard E. 1991. *Presidential Power and the Modern Presidents.* New York: Free Press.

Noelle-Neuman, Elisabeth. 1993. *The Spiral of Silence: Public Opinion—Our Social Skin.* Chicago: University of Chicago Press.

Norrander, Barbara. 1989. "Ideological Representativeness of Presidential Primary Voters." *American Journal of Political Science* 33: 570–587.

Ostling, Richard N. 1991. "What Does God Really Think About Sex?" *Time,* June 24: 48–50.

Parsons, Christi. 1997. "Constitution, Shmonstitution." *Chicago Tribune,* June 8 (Section 2): 1, 7.

People for the American Way (PAW). 1999. "Why We Support the Religious Liberty Protection Act." Available on line at www.pfaw.org/issues/rlpa/letter/shtml (cited February 5).

Perry, Michael J. 1991. *Love and Power: The Role of Religion and Morality in American Politics*. New York: Oxford University Press.

Peterson, Steven A. 1992. "Church Participation and Political Participation: The Spillover Effect." *American Politics Quarterly* 20: 123–139.

Pfeffer, Leo. 1967. *Church, State, and Freedom*. Boston: Beacon Press.

Prendergast, William B. 1999. *The Catholic Voter in American Politics*. Washington, D.C.: Georgetown University Press.

Prothro, J., and C. Grigg. 1960. "Fundamental Principles of Democracy: Bases of Agreement and Disagreement." *Journal of Politics* 22: 276–294.

Raspberry, William. 1998. "Resolving the Pro-Voucher–Anti-Voucher Squabble." *Chicago Tribune*, June 16: A12. Available on line at www.chicagotribune.com.

Rawls, John. 1993. *Political Liberalism*. New York: Columbia University Press.

Reed, Ralph. 1994. *Politically Incorrect: The Emerging Faith Factor in American Politics*. Dallas: Word.

Reichley, A. James. 1985. *Religion in American Public Life*. Washington, D.C.: Brookings.

Robbins, Thomas. 1993. "The Intensification of Church-State Conflict in the United States." *Social Compass* 40: 505–527.

Rozell, Mark J., and Clyde Wilcox. 1997. *God at the Grassroots: The Christian Right in the 1996 Elections*. Lanham, Md.: Rowman-Littlefield.

Rusher, William. 1988. *The Coming Battle for the Media: Curbing the Power of the Media Elite*. New York: William Morrow.

Savage, David C. 1993. *Turning Right: The Making of the Rehnquist Supreme Court*. New York: John Wiley and Sons.

Savage, David C., and Richard Simon. 1999. "Religious Rights: The Devil Is in the Details." *Los Angeles Times*, August 1: A1, A6.

Scalia, Antonin. 1997. "Common Law Courts in a Civil Law System: The Role of United States Federal Courts in Interpreting the Constitution and Laws." Pp. 3–48 in *A Matter of Interpretation: Federal Courts and the Law*, by Amy Guttman. Princeton: Princeton University Press.

Seelye, Katherine. 1997. "House Republicans Back Judge on Display of Ten Commandments." *New York Times*, March 5: A11.

Segers, Mary C., and Ted G. Jelen. 1998. *A Wall of Separation: Debating the Public Role of Religion*. Lanham, Md.: Rowman-Littlefield.

Sezer, L. Kent. 1995. "The Constitutional Underpinnings of the Abortion Debate." Pp. 131–176 in *Perspectives on the Politics of Abortion*, ed. Ted G. Jelen. Westport, Conn.: Praeger.

Sherry, Suzanna. 1992. "*Lee v. Weisman:* Paradox Redux." Pp. 123–153 in *1992: The Supreme Court Review*, eds. Dennis J. Hutchinson, David A. Strauss, and Geoffrey R. Stone. Chicago: University of Chicago Press.

Sigelman, Lee, Clyde Wilcox, and Emmett Buell. 1987. "An Unchanging Minority: Popular Support for the Moral Majority, 1980 and 1984." *Social Science Quarterly* 68: 876–884.

Smith, Kevin B., and Kenneth J. Meier. 1995. *The Case Against School Choice: Politics, Markets, and Fools.* Armonk, N.Y.: M. E. Sharpe.

Stark, Rodney, and Charles Y. Glock. 1968. *American Piety: The Nature of Religious Commitment.* Berkeley: University of California Press.

Steinfels, Peter. 1999. "Beliefs: A Plan to Preserve Church Ties Leaves Catholic Educators with More Questions Than Answers." *New York Times,* November 27: A7.

Tackett, Michael. 1999. "Politicians of All Stripes Tap the Well of Religion." *Chicago Tribune,* June 2: A7. Available on line at www.chicagotribune.com.

Tamney, Joseph B. Forthcoming. *The Resilience of Conservative Religion.* New York: Cambridge University Press.

Tatalovich, Raymond. 1995. *The Politics of Abortion in the United States and Canada: A Comparative Study.* Armonk, N.Y.: M. E. Sharpe.

Thiemann, Ronald. 1996. *Religion in Public Life: A Dilemma for Democracy.* Washington, D.C.: Georgetown University Press.

Tinder, Glenn. 1989. *The Political Meaning of Christianity.* Baton Rouge: Louisiana State University Press.

Tocqueville, Alexis de. 1945. *Democracy in America.* Ed. P. Bradley. 2 vols. New York: Vintage Books.

Toulmin, Stephen. 1974. *The Uses of Argument.* London: Cambridge University Press.

Tribe, Lawrence H. 1997. "Comment." Pp. 65–94 in *A Matter of Interpretation: Federal Courts and the Law,* by Amy Guttman. Princeton: Princeton University Press.

Tribe, Lawrence H., and Michael C. Dorf. 1991. *On Reading the Constitution.* Cambridge: Harvard University Press.

Tumulty, Karen. 1999. "Taking a Leap of Faith." *Time,* June 7: 58.

Verba, Sidney, Kay Lehman Schlozman, and Henry E. Brady. 1995. *Voice and Equality: Civic Voluntarism in American Politics.* Cambridge: Harvard University Press.

Vogel, Ed. 1999. "Discrimination Measure Passes." *Las Vegas Review-Journal,* May 21: 1B, 11B.

Wald, Kenneth D. 1997. *Religion and Politics in the United States.* Washington, D.C.: CQ Press.

Wald, Kenneth D., Dennis Owen, and Samuel S. Hill. 1988. "Churches as Political Communities." *American Political Science Review* 82: 531–549.

———. 1990. "Political Cohesion in Churches." *Journal of Politics* 52: 197–212.

Washington Post National Weekly Edition. 1999. "Religious Rights and Practices." August 2: 26.

Way, Frank, and Barbara Burt. 1983. "Religious Marginality and the Free Exercise Clause." *American Political Science Review* 77: 654–665.

Wayne, Stephen J. 1995. "Foreword." Pp. xi–xii in *Public Attitudes Toward Church and State,* by Ted G. Jelen and Clyde Wilcox. Armonk, N.Y.: M. E. Sharpe.

Wenz, Peter S. 1992. *Abortion Rights as Religious Freedom.* Philadelphia: Temple University Press.

Wilcox, Clyde. 1987. "Popular Support for the Moral Majority in 1980: A Second Look." *Social Science Quarterly* 68: 157–167.

_____. 1989. "The New Christian Right and the Mobilization of the Evangelicals." Pp. 139–156 in *Religion and Political Behavior in the United States,* ed. Ted G. Jelen. New York: Praeger.

_____. 1992. *God's Warriors: The Christian Right in the Twentieth Century.* Baltimore: Johns Hopkins University Press.

_____. 1996. *Onward, Christian Soldiers: The Religious Right in American Politics.* Boulder: Westview.

Wilcox, Clyde, Matthew DeBell, and Lee Sigelman. 1999. "The Second Coming of the New Christian Right: Patterns of Popular Support in 1984 and 1996." *Social Science Quarterly* 80: 181–192.

Wilcox, Clyde, Mark J. Rozell, and Roland Gunn. 1996. "Religious Coalitions in the Christian Right: The Decline of Religious Particularism." *Social Science Quarterly* 77: 543–558.

Wills, Garry. 1990. *Under God: Religion and American Politics.* New York: Simon and Schuster.

Witcover, Jules. 1977. *Marathon.* New York: Random House.

Witte, John. 1999. *Religion and the American Constitutional Experiment.* Boulder: Westview.

Wood, James W. 1990. *The First Freedom: Religion and the Bill of Rights.* Waco, Tex.: Baylor University, J. M. Dawson Institute of Church-State Relations.

Wrinkle, Robert D., Joseph Stewart, Jr., and J. L. Polinard. 1999. "Public School Quality, Private Schools, and Race." *American Journal of Political Science* 43: 1248–1263.

Zaller, John R. 1992. *The Nature and Origins of Mass Opinion.* New York: Cambridge University Press.

Zwier, Robert. 1989. *Coalition Strategies of Religious Interest Groups.* Pp. 171–186 in *Religion and Political Behavior in the United States,* ed. Ted G. Jelen. New York: Praeger.

Index